IIM
AHMEDABAD
BUSINESS BOOKS

HOW TO MAKE THE
RIGHT DECISION

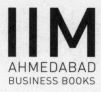

IIM
AHMEDABAD
BUSINESS BOOKS

HOW TO MAKE THE RIGHT DECISION

ARNAB K. LAHA

RANDOM HOUSE INDIA

Published by Random House India in 2015
1

Random House Publishers India Pvt Ltd
7th Floor, Infinity Tower C, DLF Cyber City
Gurgaon – 122002
Haryana

Random House Group Limited
20 Vauxhall Bridge Road
London SW1V 2SA
United Kingdom

978 81 8400 162 4

Typeset in Sabon by R. Ajith Kumar

Printed and bound in India by Replika Press Pvt. Ltd

A PENGUIN RANDOM HOUSE COMPANY

CONTENTS

ACKNOWLEDGEMENTS

The present book started off from a request of Prof. Samir K. Barua, the then director of IIM Ahmedabad, to write a book on business analytics for practising managers. While I agreed to his suggestion tentatively, I soon figured out the difficulty of communicating a highly technical subject in simple language to an audience without the appropriate technical background. I decided to adopt a storytelling approach, with each story highlighting the use of analytics in a certain business area. The initial progress was very slow. In this phase, Chiki Sarkar, who was then coordinating this book project from the Random House side, made it a point to call me up quite frequently to encourage me and helped me with many a tip on how to make progress with the manuscript. One of her tips was to seek the involvement of a talented student for the project. While

I kept this suggestion in mind, I felt that it would be nearly impossible to get an IIMA student interested in a book project given the students' packed schedules.

And then came along Vinay Bhaskar, without whose unstinting support this book would not have seen the light of day. He was then a participant of the one-year full-time Post Graduate Programme for Executives (PGPX) at IIMA and had done extremely well in my courses. One day he approached me to explore the possibility of doing a project course with me. I broached with him the idea of helping me with this book and sent him the drafts that I had made. Vinay worked on these rough drafts and using his enormous creativity chiselled them into the chapters that you read in this book. In my opinion, it would have been most appropriate for him to be the co-author. However, being a self-effacing person with great respect for his teachers, Vinay has graciously left the formal authorship of the book to me. But in my mind he remains the co-author of this work.

I would also like to thank Milee Ashwarya and Radhika Marwah from Random House for their patience and support in bringing this book project to its conclusion. A special note of thanks is due to Richa Burman for her excellent editing.

CHAPTER 1

IN THE EYES OF THE LENDER

Sachin is a chartered accountant by profession and works for a reputed multinational firm in India. Recently, he has placed a request for a credit card with a leading Indian bank. After a long wait of six weeks, he receives a notification from the bank that his application has been rejected. Sachin is taken aback by the decision. He earns a decent salary and has furnished all the financial details to the bank, and yet his application has been rejected.

In another interesting instance, Apoorva Bank has recently approved a factory loan to a small-sized firm in Gurgaon while it declined any credit to a mid-sized business operating across India and with revenues twenty-five times the revenues of the small-sized firm.

In the two instances, the banks have used some

criteria for selection in granting or declining the credit card/loan to their customers. But what are those criteria and how does a bank decide that it should or should not grant credit to a particular individual or business?

The answer lies in Credit Scoring, which is at the heart of any credit decision-making. A good selection criterion aims at avoiding losses and hence tries to assess the borrower's risk. By selecting customers who are likely to repay the debt, a bank reduces its chances of suffering a loss on the loans granted.

The practice is not new. In the olden days, when a village moneylender would grant credit to a farmer, he would ask for some collateral (crop produce, house papers, jewellery, and so on). In case these were not available, he would assess the farmer's repaying capacity based on his past experience with him, the size of his land, be it owned or rented, the size of his family to assess his expenses, etc. Let's call these factors 'decision variables'. Then, based on his expert judgement he would decide to grant or not grant him a loan.

Now consider a hypothetical case where instead of a few villagers, he has to deal with thousands of borrowers at his shop every day asking for credit. Expert decision-making on a case-by-case basis in this scenario would be inefficient and may generate loans of poor quality. He may also lose some borrowers to other moneylenders, in case he takes too much time to take the decision. What can a moneylender do? Can he improve his decision-making capabilities? Yes, if he can somehow give a ranking to each borrower, based on certain fixed decision variables, and then approve the loan to only those who are above a certain cut-off. To illustrate, if he has ten borrowers lined up for credit, he may number them 1 to 10, 1 being the best and 10 being the worst in terms of potential repayment behaviour. Now, if the moneylender wants to give credit to only 30 per cent of the potential borrowers, he will pick the customers numbered 1, 2 and 3 for the same.

This is what banks do when they have to scan thousands of credit applications month after month.

THE CREDIT SCORE

Let's bring our friend Sachin back into the picture. Assume that the bank uses the following decision variables (characteristics or factors) in assessing a borrower's repayment capacity: age, income and employment status.

TABLE 1.1: A Sample Scorecard

Decision Variable	Range	Score Points
Age	Upto 25	70
	25–40	100
	Above 40	120
Income (per month)	Upto 20,000	50
	20,000–50,000	80
	Above 50,000	100
Employment Status	Unemployed	20
	Self-Employed	50
	Private	80
	Government	100
	Others	60

If Sachin's age is 28 and he draws a monthly income of Rs 30,000 working in a private sector, he will get a score of 260 (100 + 80 + 80 as mapped from Table 1.1). The higher the score, the better the chances that he will repay the debt. Similarly, the lower the score, the lower his chances of being able to repay the loan. Hence, the bank will compare the score against its predetermined cut-off and will decide on whether credit should be granted or not. The cut-off is decided based on the bank's appetite for risk and its strategy in terms of growth, targeting, and so on.

The next question to ask is how does a bank come up with the score points for particular decision variables and how does it choose the score cut-off?

This is where data analytics and statistical techniques play a significant role.

THE CREDIT SCORE PROCESS

A three-stage process is followed in assessing the borrower's chances of defaulting on the loan and this assessment is then used for granting him a loan or not.

Stage 1: Preparing the Data

Data lies at the heart of Credit Score development. In its simplest form, data includes a list of the existing customers (see tip below on 'reject inference'), together with the customers' characteristics as of the date when their loan/credit was approved. In addition, an indicator is created to flag the customer who has been behaving well on repayment terms unlike another who has defaulted on the loan.

Figure 1.1 highlights the data preparation for the model development process starting in, say, January 2010. Here, one has chosen to track all the approved

FIGURE 1.1: Data Preparation Period

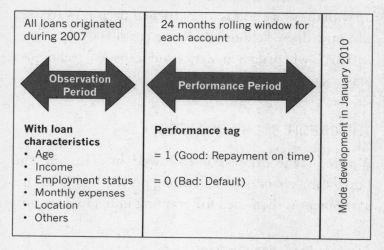

loans of a bank from 2007 for a period of twenty-four months. The period from which approved customers are chosen is called the 'observation period' and the period for which the repayment behaviour is tracked is called the 'performance period'. A performance tag of 1 (Good) or 0 (Bad) is calculated for each customer during the performance period.

The definition of a performance tag depends upon the characteristic of the loan product. For shorter-term loans, say car loan or student loan, one may decide to use the shorter window of performance and tag a borrower as Bad if he misses two consecutive payments during the performance period. For some other products, say, home loan, one may decide to tag a borrower as Bad only if he misses six consecutive payments.

One can also exercise flexibility in choosing the starting date and the length of the observation period. It all depends upon how much data one wants to track and how recent the data should be.

While looking at only existing customers is convenient, one should not forget the accounts rejected in the past since it will bring in the bias due to past strategy through which only a subset of accounts had been approved.

To overcome this, a technique called 'reject inference' is used to estimate the behaviour of rejected accounts. Ideally, both existing and rejected accounts should form part of the modelling dataset.

Please ensure that the performance period is used only to tag good or bad behaviour. No other loan characteristic should come from this period.

Stage 2: Developing the Model

Model development forms a critical step as the collected data in Stage 1 is used to generate the score points for each loan characteristic that is important in predicting repayment behaviour.

While various techniques are available to model such behaviour, the 'logistic regression' method is used most often. The name derives from the use of the logistic function in the Regression Technique.[1] The technique is used primarily to predict the categorical behaviour (behaviour or outcome with a limited number of possibilities) using the independent factors that one considers critical to such behaviour. In our case, it is being used to predict the repayment behaviour of a borrower (taking two values: Good behaviour and Bad behaviour) based on the borrower's characteristics at the time of loan application. The underlying assumption is that the past predicts the future. If, in the past, certain characteristics have led to a particular behaviour or outcome, the occurrence of those characteristics in the future may lead to the same behaviour.

Once the logistic regression technique is applied to the data at hand, one may get the result that only age, income and employment status matter in borrowers' behaviour to repay the loan over time (these are termed 'statistically significant variables'), and that other characteristics such as monthly expenses, location, etc., can be ignored.

The model also assigns the relative importance (weight) to each significant characteristic. For example, age may get a weight of +0.9. A positive sign implies that the higher the age, the better the chances of the borrower not defaulting. If the sign were negative, the opposite relationship would hold.

Weights for each of the significant variables can be converted into an easy-to-use scorecard as depicted in Table 1.1. The final score for a borrower would be the sum total of all the score points a borrower gathers for each of the characteristics.

While various measures are used to check the quality of a score, one such measure is called Divergence. Once we get the scores for all the borrowers in our data, we can plot the Good/Bad flag against the score to see how effective our score is in separating good versus bad accounts.

A good score would have minimal overlap between the areas for good accounts and bad accounts. A higher overlap means that for a particular score there are both good and bad accounts, and hence the score did not do a great job in separating the two.

FIGURE 1.2: Divergence Method

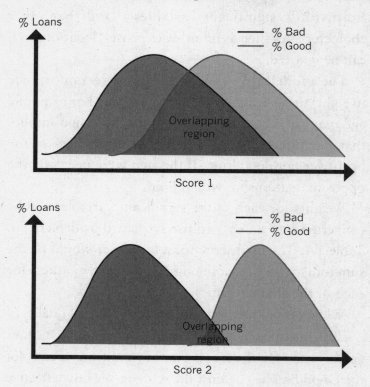

In Figure 1.2, Score 2 is better than Score 1 in terms of separating good versus bad repayment behaviour.

Please note that there will always be some overlap between the two areas. It is practically impossible to have no overlap.

Stage 3: Choosing the Score Cut-Off and Leveraging It for Credit Decision-Making

Once the score is developed, the next task is to choose the score cut-off. If any new loan application gets a score above the cut-off, the loan is granted, otherwise the loan is rejected.

Choosing the cut-off is quite an involved process, and various factors such as the risk appetite of the business, business strategy (whether the focus is on capturing market share or on growing profitable accounts), and so on, need to be taken into account. As an illustration, we will consider a simple case where the risk appetite—measured in terms of the percentage of bad loans a business is ready to tolerate—is the only criterion for choosing the cut-off.

TABLE 1.2: Distribution of Accounts across Different Scores

Score Range (Col. 1)	Loan Accounts (Col. 2)	No. of Bad (Col. 3)	Cumulative No. of Loan Accounts (Col. 4)	Cumulative No. of Bad (Col. 5)	Percentage of Cumulative Bad (Col. 6)
300+	40	1	40	1	2.5%
200–300	30	5	70	6	8.6%
100–200	20	6	90	12	13.3%
0–100	10	8	100	20	20%
Total	100	20	100	20	20%

Let's assume that there are 100 loan accounts that have been scored through the scoring logic. Table 1.2 lists the distribution of accounts across score ranges as well as the number of bad accounts in each score range. For example, there are 40 accounts with scores above 300 and of those 1 is bad.

The table also shows the cumulative number of loan accounts (column 4) and cumulative number of bad accounts (column 5) above a particular score range. For example, the score range 200–300 has cumulative loan accounts numbered 70 (40 + 30) and the cumulative bad accounts are 6 (1 + 5). The last column is just a percentage of cumulative bad loans above a score range: column 5/column 4 (in this case, 6/70).

Now, if a business has an appetite for around 14 per cent bad accounts, it may choose to approve anyone above a score of 100. While if it is risk-averse and will tolerate only 3 per cent bad accounts, it will choose a score cut-off of 300.

Apparently, Sachin's application got rejected because his credit score wasn't above or equal to the bank's risk appetite. The bank has historically seen profiles, akin to Sachin's, defaulting on loans in proportions that it cannot tolerate and hence is unwilling to extend him the credit.

Sachin may apply for and receive credit from other banks, but those banks may also charge a higher interest rate to cover their risk. But that's another story.

SUMMARY

Scoring forms an important tool in new-age credit-risk analytics. While various techniques are available to develop the score, logistic regression is the most popular among them. The technique dwells on the assumption that the past predicts the future. If certain features in the past have led to a particular outcome, the occurrence of the same features in the future may again lead to the same outcome. In this chapter, we learnt how scoring can be used to predict the repayment behaviour of a credit borrower. The score thus developed is called a credit score.

YOU MUST ALSO KNOW

➢ As an alternative to building an internal score, one may buy the score from CIBIL (Credit Information Bureau Limited), India's new credit bureau. This score would look at individual's/commercial

---

performance across its loans with all the lenders. Such a score is called a 'bureau score'.

➢ A lender is required by law to offer reasons for rejecting an application if a score has been used in the decision-making process. These reasons are called 'adverse action' reasons and are based on the worst characteristics that form a part of scoring logic for which a borrower got a low score and hence was denied credit.

CHAPTER 2

WHERE THE MONEY LIES

Trendz Fashion is a women's apparel store chain in north India, headquartered in New Delhi. The firm has a production factory in Gurgaon and employs 100 labourers working on five machines that produce garments. Recently, due to an increased demand for its much-in-vogue designs, the factory has been running at full capacity. Most of its orders are pending and the firm risks losing customers to its competitors. Vandana Sahni, the managing director of the firm, is contemplating purchasing five more machines to meet the demand. This would also require hiring five additional workers and renting a small space adjacent to the factory. Her dilemma is whether the demand is enough to warrant the purchase of new machines. Moreover, is this increase in demand going to last long enough and be stable over time? What should be the basis of her financial decision? As an alternative, could she invest her money in the stock market and earn better returns?

As another example, an oil exploration company is in the midst of deciding whether to bid for the drilling rights at a newfound oil site. The drilling requires an investment of Rs 10 crore. There is a chance that the drilling may not result in any oil, in which case the project will be a failure. If the company does find oil, the question will be about the amount of reserves present. Another important factor is the price of the oil. If prices fall over time, the company will lose money. The different alternatives are troubling the management team who have to take the decision in the next forty-eight hours.

Decisions such as these are termed 'capital budgeting' in the parlance of corporate finance, and form the backbone of any business—from a small-sized firm to a multi-billion-dollar business like General Electric.

THE BASIS OF EVALUATION

The basis of evaluating any project is quite intuitive in nature. Any project brings associated benefits and costs over its useful life (generally termed 'economic life'). The objective of any project evaluation, then, is to analyse whether the benefits exceed the costs by an extent that would not be possible in any other alternative project or investment.

So, there are three factors for evaluating a project over its useful life:

1. Cash inflows
2. Cash outflows
3. Opportunity cost of invested money (also called opportunity cost of capital)

The first two factors are almost self-explanatory. For Trendz Fashion, assuming the useful life of the machines to be five years, cash inflow would be the cash generated through sales over a period of five years. Similarly, all the cash expenses, such as salary of workers, raw material consumption, electricity bills and rent of the facility, etc., would be cash outflows, again considered for a period of five years.

The third factor, opportunity cost of money, measures the return on money if it were used for an alternative project/investment of equal risk. Assume that as an alternative to investing in five new machines, Vandana could invest her money in the stock market, purchasing stocks of companies with risk similar to Trendz Fashion's proposal of new investments. Let's say that those stocks give a return of 15 per cent per annum on her investment, then the opportunity cost for Vandana would be 15 per cent return. In other words, opportunity cost is the cost associated with forgoing the next best alternative, which is investment in stocks with similar risk in Vandana's case.

The concept of opportunity cost of capital is valid only if we compare projects of equivalent risk. Comparing returns on projects of different risks would be unfair. One can gamble and earn more money than by investing in a project. But are the two the same?

If project financing requires borrowing money, in addition to the investor's own money, the opportunity cost of capital has to also consider the borrowing cost.

The cost of capital would then be the weighted average of borrowing cost and the opportunity cost of one's own money, the weights being the percentage contribution of each type of fund (borrowed or own money) to total money.

THE MECHANICS OF EVALUATION

The mechanics of evaluating a project over its useful life is slightly complicated. In essence, it's a four-step process as illustrated in Figure 2.1.

FIGURE 2.1: Steps Involved in Evaluating a Project through NPV Criteria

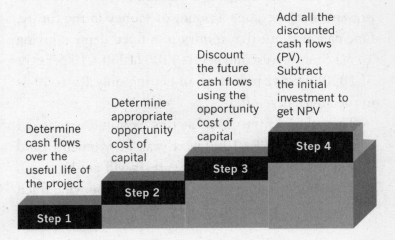

Determine cash flows over the useful life of the project

Determine appropriate opportunity cost of capital

Discount the future cash flows using the opportunity cost of capital

Add all the discounted cash flows (PV). Subtract the initial investment to get NPV

Step 1

Step 2

Step 3

Step 4

We have introduced elements of the first two steps earlier in this chapter. Let's now see how we use them as we proceed to steps 3 and 4.

Before proceeding, we need to understand the useful concept of 'discounting' and, associated with it, the notion of 'present value'. Complex though the terms may sound, these are quite intuitive in nature and we use them even in our daily lives.

Suppose, as part of a deal I offer to pay you Rs 1000 this year. Alternatively, I offer to pay you Rs 1000 next year. Which offer would you choose? The answer seems obvious. One would most likely choose to receive Rs 1000 this year rather than next year. Why is that so? It is because one attaches more value to the money at present than the same amount of money in the future. One can also put that money in a fixed deposit giving 10 per cent interest and get Rs 1100 (1000 + 10 per cent of 1000) next year, instead of getting only Rs 1000 as in the alternative offer.

The other way to look at this example is that if I offer to give you Rs 1000 next year, how much would it be worth to you today? For sure, it will not be worth Rs 1000 but less than that. The fact that you will attach a lower value today to money received in the future implies that you are 'discounting' the future value. The value thus calculated is called the present value, or PV, of the future money.

The exact discounted or present value depends upon the applied 'discount rate'. This rate equals the return foregone if one accepts receiving money in the future rather than receiving the money at present. So using 10 per cent as interest foregone in the example above, Rs 1000 would be equivalent to Rs 909.09 today (1000/ (1 + 10 per cent)). This is because if you invest Rs 909.09 in a bank's fixed deposit giving 10 per cent interest for one year, you will receive Rs 1000 (Rs 909.09 + Rs 90.91 interest) at maturity. If the interest rate were higher, say 20 per cent, the PV would have shrunk to Rs 833.33.

The other key point to note in relation to PV is that the farther into the future the money is received, the lower its value will be today. So, a PV of Rs 1000 received two years from now would be lower than the PV of Rs 1000 received next year.

The general formula to calculate PV is summarized in Figure 2.2.

Now that we have understood the concepts of discounting and PV, we can resume our discussion about Step 3, valuing a project as shown in Figure 2.1.

FIGURE 2.2: Calculating the Present Value

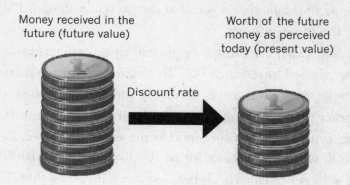

Money received in the future (future value)

Worth of the future money as perceived today (present value)

Discount rate

Let r be the applied discount rate

PV of Rs X received n years from now = $x/(1+r\%)^n$

As discussed before, a project would generate the cash inflows and require cash outflows for the duration of its useful life. In Step 3, we would discount all those cash flows and calculate the PV of those cash flows for each of the years using the appropriate discount rate. For the purpose of project evaluation, the opportunity cost of capital is used as the discount rate.

In Step 4, PVs calculated for each of the years are added to find the PV of the entire project. From this PV of the project, if one subtracts the initial investment required to start the project, one would get 'net present value', or NPV.

Once we have calculated the NPV of the project, the final decision to undertake the project or not becomes quite simple. If the NPV is greater than zero, undertake the project; if the NPV is less than zero, reject the project.

Figure 2.3 illustrates the mechanics of deriving the NPV and Example 2.1 details it for Trendz Fashion.

FIGURE 2.3: The Mechanics of Deriving the NPV of a Project

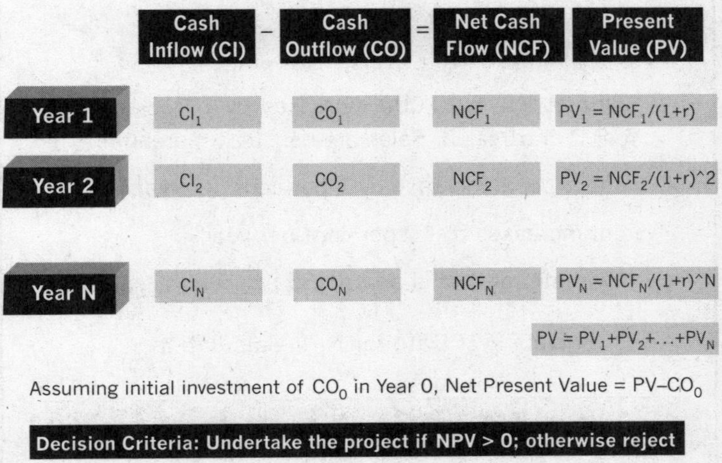

	Cash Inflow (CI)	−	Cash Outflow (CO)	=	Net Cash Flow (NCF)	Present Value (PV)
Year 1	CI_1		CO_1		NCF_1	$PV_1 = NCF_1/(1+r)$
Year 2	CI_2		CO_2		NCF_2	$PV_2 = NCF_2/(1+r)^2$
Year N	CI_N		CO_N		NCF_N	$PV_N = NCF_N/(1+r)^N$

$$PV = PV_1 + PV_2 + \ldots + PV_N$$

Assuming initial investment of CO_0 in Year 0, Net Present Value = $PV - CO_0$

Decision Criteria: Undertake the project if NPV > 0; otherwise reject

EXAMPLE 2.1: NPV Calculation of Trendz Fashion

The cash flow model is depicted in the table below.

Model Details

➢ Five machines are purchased at a cost of Rs 50,000 each, making it an initial investment of Rs 2,50,000.

➢ Five workers are hired at the cost of Rs 4000 per month, totalling an additional monthly expenditure of Rs 20,000.

Model Assumptions

➢ Sales of Rs 5,20,000 increases by 10 per cent for Year 2 and Year 3. Sales are constant thereafter.

➢ Labour costs increase by 5 per cent per year.

➢ Rent increases by 10 per cent per year.

➢ Raw material cost is around 35 per cent of sales.

TABLE 2.1: Data for NPV Calculation

(in Rs)

	Year 0	Year 1	Year 2	Year 3	Year 4	Year 5
Initial Investment	2,50,000					
Sale (A)		5,20,000	5,72,000	6,29,200	6,29,200	6,29,200
Raw Material Cost (B)		1,82,000	2,00,200	2,20,220	2,20,220	2,20,220

	Year 0	Year 1	Year 2	Year 3	Year 4	Year 5
Labour Cost (C)		2,40,000	2,52,000	2,64,600	2,77,830	2,91,722
Electricity Cost (D)		10,000	10,000	10,000	10,000	10,000
Net Cash Flow (NCF=A–B–C–D)		68,000	87,800	1,10,180	94,530	77,977
Present Value at the Discount Rate of 15%		59,130	66,389	72,445	54,048	38,768
Total Present Value	2,90,781					
NPV	40,781					

In the above table, Vandana Sahni makes an initial investment of Rs 2,50,000 in purchasing 5 new machines. The machines are expected to generate incremental sales for the next five years as highlighted in the second row. To generate these sales, Vandana will have to spend money on raw material, labour and electricity, as depicted by the next three rows. As a next step, net cash flow calculates the difference of sales over the total costs for five years. The last two steps then involve discounting the net cash flow using the 15 per cent discount rate to get the PV of cash flows and then subtracting the initial investment of Rs 2,50,000 to get the NPV.

Since the calculations generate positive NPV, Vandana Sahni should invest Rs 2,50,000 in the new machines.

Please note that not all sales made during a period will result in cash inflow to the company in that period. So, if a sale is made on credit, say, in Year 1 and cash is received only in Year 2, such sales should be calculated only in Year 2.

Please note that issues of taxes, working capital requirement and disposable value of machines at the end of Year 5 are ignored in these calculations. These factors play a critical role in NPV assessment.

Moreover, NPV is just one of the criteria for project evaluation. Other criteria include internal rate of return and payback calculations.[1]

EVALUATING UNCERTAINTIES

Besides NPV assessment, a sound investment decision would also be based on a careful evaluation of the embedded uncertainties in a project and their impact on the NPV.

These uncertainties are in the nature of 'What if' questions that one should have answers to and be comfortable with, before committing oneself to the project. Extending the details of Example 2.1 for Trendz Fashion,

1. What if the sales levels in years 1 and 2 turn out to be lower than what was expected by Vandana Sahni because of a change in fashion or due to intense competition? Will the project still hold its worth?

2. What if the labour cost increases by 10 per cent year on year instead of 5 per cent, as assumed in the NPV calculation above?

3. What if there is a shortage of raw-material supply specific to the apparel produced by Trendz Fashion that increases the price of raw material by 30 per cent? By how much will it reduce the NPV?

The cash flow model in Example 2.1 is based on the *expected* values of the factors contributing to the NPV. To elaborate, if there is a 20 per cent chance that sales in Year 1 would be Rs 8,00,000 and an 80 per cent chance that sales would be Rs 4,50,000, the expected value would be the weighted average of the two, the weights being the chance associated with each value. In this case, the expected value is 20 per cent × 8,00,000

+ 80 per cent × 4,50,000 = Rs 5,20,000. However, as highlighted in question 1 above, if one looks only at the expected value, there is a risk that the actual NPV may turn out to be different from the one calculated because the actual value of a factor in the cash flow model (sales in this case) has deviated from the expected value.

To evaluate the impact of such uncertainties on a project's health, there are three primary techniques available to a decision maker, namely, sensitivity analysis, scenario analysis and Monte Carlo simulations.

Sensitivity Analysis

The primary objective of this analysis is to gauge the sensitivity of the NPV of a project due to key factors in the financial calculations as highlighted in Example 2.1. This is achieved by calculating the NPV for the best-case and worst-case values for each of those factors.

For example, sales in Year 1 have a best-case value of Rs 8,00,000 and a worst-case value of Rs 4,50,000. Recalculating, for the best case, we get a total PV of Rs 7,30,620, and in the worst case, the total PV drops to Rs 1,31,679. Note that the project is not worth undertaking *as is* in the worst-case scenario since the NPV is negative and there is an 80 per cent chance that this can happen.

Based on this analysis, a decision maker will try to analyse if certain other measures can be taken, such as expanding the production to different types of garments from those in vogue today if sales in Year 1 turn out to be lower than expected. If such measures are feasible and bring the NPV back to a positive level, the decision maker will undertake the project. This is an example of 'Real Option', where there is the flexibility to change the course of the project if the results are not as expected. More on real options later.

A key point to note is that sensitivity analysis looks at the impact of each factor in isolation and ignores the interrelationships between factors. To exemplify, if lower sales in Year 1 are due to macroeconomic factors, this may also impact the cost of labour in a favourable way. So, while on the one hand the NPV will reduce due to lower sales, reduced cost of labour would tend to increase the NPV. Such interactions are ignored in sensitivity analysis. This is a serious limitation of this type of analysis.

Scenario Analysis

The limitation highlighted above can be countered to an extent if we undertake a scenario analysis. The primary idea is to create certain scenarios or situations that are plausible and impact each of the factors in a model in a coherent manner. Such scenarios take into account the interactions across factors while evaluating the impact of uncertainties on the NPV.

For example, Vandana Sahni may consider two scenarios based on the growth potential of the market and the raw-material market conditions.

SCENARIO 1: HIGH GROWTH, LOW COST

This is a scenario where the fashion apparel market overall would experience high growth (20 per cent year on year) in the next five years. Trendz Fashion expects to beat the market and gain 25 per cent increase in sales each year as against the base case (original) scenario of 10 per cent growth in sales. This high growth would also entail higher labour cost, around 15 per cent increase each year, as against the 5 per cent originally assumed in the model. The cost of raw material is expected to be at a medium level and around 20 per cent of sales due to the new sources (say, Indonesia) from where Vandana can possibly import it.

SCENARIO 2: LOW GROWTH, STABLE COST

This is a scenario where the fashion apparel market overall would experience low growth (5 per cent year on year) in the next five years. Trendz Fashion expects to gain only 5 per cent increase in sales year on year as against the base case (original) scenario of 10 per cent growth in sales. This low growth would benefit Trendz Fashion in terms of lower labour costs, around 2 per cent increase each year, as against the 5 per cent originally assumed in the model. The cost of raw material is expected to be stable at around 35 per cent of sales due to the new sources (Indonesia) failing to supply the raw materials due.

The expected NPV for each of the scenarios is calculated to evaluate the impact of the interrelationships of the factors in each scenario.

MONTE CARLO SIMULATIONS

While scenario analysis is an improvement on sensitivity analysis in terms of capturing interactions across factors, it is still limited to the number of scenarios being considered by a decision maker. There is a risk that a decision maker inadvertently fails to consider a probable and critical scenario and hence errs while taking a decision on the project. To minimize the chance of any such risk, Monte Carlo Simulations provide an excellent tool to consider all possible combinations of the factors in evaluating the NPV of a project.[2] Monte

Carlo simulation techniques provide the user with all the possible outcomes, together with the probability of their occurrences.

Monte Carlo simulations[3] require the use of a spreadsheet-like software, such as Microsoft Excel, or a statistical software package like Minitab, SAS, R, etc., wherein the user feeds all the possible values of key factors together with the probability of the occurrence

FIGURE 2.4: Techniques to Evaluate the Impact of Uncertainties in a Project

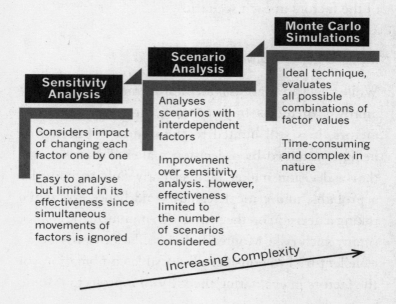

Monte Carlo Simulations

Ideal technique, evaluates all possible combinations of factor values

Time-consuming and complex in nature

Scenario Analysis

Analyses scenarios with interdependent factors

Improvement over sensitivity analysis. However, effectiveness limited to the number of scenarios considered

Sensitivity Analysis

Considers impact of changing each factor one by one

Easy to analyse but limited in its effectiveness since simultaneous movements of factors is ignored

Increasing Complexity

of each value (in case of discrete variables) or feeds the possible distribution of the factors (in case of continuous variables). The software then generates the values for each of the factors iteratively. Each iteration is called a 'simulation run' and provides a possible combination of the values of the factors considered in the model. Thereafter the NPV is calculated for each iteration. By running several iterations (at times 100,000 or more), one gets the possible NPVs for each combination of factors from which the distribution of the NPV, the expected NPV and quantities such as the 'value at risk' can be calculated.

INTRODUCING REAL OPTIONS

Real options, if available, enhance the value of a project beyond the NPV calculations highlighted in the previous section. Real options provide the flexibility to a decision maker to change the course of the project if things don't fall in place as expected.

If Vandana Sahni finds that the demand for her particular style of apparel is falling after she has invested in the machines, does she have an exit option? Can she sell off the machines at a fair price easily or can those machines be utilized to produce other styles of apparel?

If the machines are designed for a specific style of apparel, then they cannot be put to an alternative use. Moreover, if they were costly, then finding a buyer in the second-hand market would prove difficult. In either case, investment in such machines will not have provided much flexibility to Vandana in terms of exit options.

On the other hand, if there were more options to use the machines or if it were easier to find a buyer in case she decided to sell the machines, then the value of investing in this project would be greater due to the 'real options' provided by the machines.

Real options not only provide a choice for exit, they provide an opportunity to expand as well. In another scenario, if the space Vandana has rented for these five machines can also be utilized for setting up two more machines, in case the market grows phenomenally beyond expectations, then she will not have to bother to rent another space at that critical time. The set-up time needed to catch up with the increase in demand would be considerably less. This is a real option to expand.

SUMMARY

Financial decisions involving alternative choices pose a significant challenge to the investor. Who in this world

Real option is just an option and not an obligation. A decision maker may choose to exercise that option when the time comes. This flexibility is what generates additional value for the project.

would not like to have the best return on an investment? Decisions related to heavy investments in particular pose considerable financial risk to any organization. The concepts and techniques discussed in this chapter, such as discounting, opportunity cost, net present value, scenario analysis, etc., can help decision makers evaluate the possibilities of various outcomes. The goal is to know the unknowns 'as much as possible' and take informed decisions involving money.

YOU MUST ALSO KNOW

➢ Discounting cash flow techniques can also be used to value the overall firm. This is what potential buyers of firms use when they bid during mergers and acquisitions. Here, all the projected cash flows due to various current and potential projects of the firm are discounted to get the overall value of the firm.

➤ While real options look at the options related to the changing course of a project, there are financial options that provide flexibility to either buy or sell a financial product at a predetermined price by a particular date.

CHAPTER 3

IN THE WORLD OF RISKS

'Risk is a part of God's game, alike for men and nations.'
— WARREN BUFFET

In personal and business spheres alike, the presence of risk impacts the value of the alternatives that one chooses from. While the final choice depends upon the level of affinity one shows towards risk, everyone aims to minimize the impact of risk. As Warren mentioned once 'Risk comes from not knowing what you're doing', hence risk assessment and management is a critical aspect of any decision that involves uncertainty.

In simple terms, risk is the possibility of a loss due to certain action (or inaction). Risk management is a process of identifying such risks, measuring them and taking appropriate counteractions to reduce their impact.

More formally, the International Organization for Standardization (ISO) defines risk as the effect of 'uncertainties on objectives'. These uncertainties include events that may or may not happen and uncertainties that arise due to a lack of information. Moreover, the definition covers not only the negative impacts of risk on objectives but also the positive ones.

ISO is a worldwide federation of national standards bodies, at present comprising 164 members (as of 2013), one in each country.

The object of ISO is to promote the development of standardization and related activities in the world with a view to facilitating international exchange of goods and services.

The results of ISO's technical work are published as International Standards. ISO standard 31000 deals with risk and risk management.

In the financial world, risk is defined as the variation in the expected return from any investment. Consider two alternative investments: investing in real estate and investing in stocks. Let's say real-estate investment generates an annual expected return of 10 per cent for an investor while investment in stocks generates an annual expected return of 15 per cent. Which one would you choose?

If you base your decision only on average returns, then the answer is clear: invest in stocks since the returns are higher. But are you ignoring something while making this choice? What about the risk in these investments? Is there equal probability of getting returns from either investment in any given year?

Let's look at an example: suppose real-estate investment in the past twenty years has been giving investors either 8 per cent or 12 per cent annual return on investment. Moreover, both levels of returns have occurred for an equal number of years, implying that either return is equally likely for an investor. If one calculates average or expected return over the twenty-year period, one would arrive at a figure of 10 per cent. Similarly, suppose investment in stocks has equally likely return values of 5 per cent and 25 per cent, giving it an average (expected) return of 15 per cent.

(Please note that we have considered only two levels of returns for either investment in order to keep the illustration simple. In a real scenario, the returns would follow a continuous pattern. They could be anywhere between a very high negative and a very high positive figure.)

Now, since the variation in returns for stocks is higher than for variation in returns in real estate, an investor who avoids taking risks will choose real-estate investment and would be satisfied with the lower average returns of 10 per cent. She is guaranteeing herself a return of 8 per cent while there is a possibility of returns dropping to 5 per cent if she chooses stocks. On the other hand, a lover of risks would prefer investing in stocks as it gives higher average returns.

An investor would always find herself facing the trade-off between risk and return and hence, in addition to average returns, she also looks at the variation in the returns over the year while making an investment decision. The same is illustrated in Figure 3.1.

Figure 3.1 plots average return on investment on the X (horizontal) axis and risk (captured through variation) on the Y axis. The entire risk–return space on the graph is divided into four regions: Region 1: high risk, low return; Region 2: high risk, high return; Region 3: low risk, high return; and Region 4: low risk, low return. In addition, four investment choices are considered in

FIGURE 3.1: Risk–Return Trade-Off

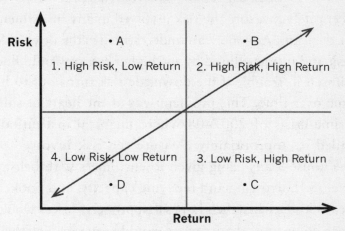

An investor would prefer investment B over A, C over B, C over D and D over A; however, the real dilemma would be in deciding between B and D and that is where the risk–return trade-off lies.

this space, namely, A, B, C and D, each belonging to one region.

Given a choice, one would prefer investment B to A (since returns are higher but risk is the same) or C to B (risk is lower but returns are the same). Also, one would prefer C over D or D over A. Why? The real challenge would be choosing between B and D since risk or return levels are not the same in both. Lovers of risk would choose B while risk-averse investors would prefer D and be satisfied with lower expected returns.

The critical aspect of risk–return trade-off is to accurately measure the risk involved in any investment or decision. Anyone who underestimates the downside risk and just gets lured by the higher return would find himself in trouble if the downside risk turns out to be true over time. This problem was at the heart of sub-prime crisis of 2007–08 where financial institutions failed to appropriately measure the risk involved in the house loans being given to customers with below-average borrowing and repaying capacity, and booked heavy losses when their hopes that property prices would keep going up and borrowers would keep repaying their debt were dashed.

FINANCIAL RISKS

Financial risk is a broad term for a variety of risks that impact the monetary value of any type of financial decision. Broadly, there are four ways in which financial risk can manifest itself, namely, credit risk, market risk, operational risk and liquidity risk.

Credit risk arises when there is a risk of a borrower defaulting on his agreed-upon payment, thus resulting in a loss of interest and principal to the creditor. Managing credit risk remains one of the biggest challenges for village moneylenders and modern-day financial institutions alike. The only solace is that modern-day institutions now have better access to sophisticated statistical modelling techniques to predict the probability of default by a customer.

Market risk refers to the loss in value of the investment due to market factors, such as interest rate fluctuation, currency exchange rate fluctuation, and so on. The simplest example is that of fluctuating value of investment in the stock market due to demand/supply conditions, economy behaviour, market sentiments, etc. If you have invested in stocks, you are subject to market risk because the market value of your stocks may change every second!

The other two types of financial risks are easier to explain. While operational risk refers to the risk arising due to the execution of business function and covers broad areas such as risk due to fraud, environmental risk, legal risk, reputation risk, etc., liquidity risk arises if the asset/investment cannot be sold easily in the market in case an adverse situation arises and the investor wishes to minimize loss. For example, investment in property/land is less liquid than investment in gold or fixed deposits.

All four types of risk endanger the value of the

investment and thus require prudent and comprehensive mechanisms through which they can be managed or mitigated.

RISK FRAMEWORKS

While businesses and financial institutions may develop their own internal mechanisms/methods to effectively assess and manage risks, they are also guided by the variety of standard risk frameworks, created by either regulation, government or international bodies with an aim to standardize practices. Risk framework, in a broad sense, refers to a set of guiding principles through which risk can be assessed and managed. The primary among such frameworks are the ISO and Basel frameworks.

ISO is the world's largest developer and publisher of international standards. It has more than 18,500 standards, covering activities ranging from traditional ones such as agriculture and construction to the more advanced sectors of information and technology and medical devices.

Risk management guidelines are published in ISO 31000: 2009 standards. These standards can be used by any public, private or community enterprise, association, group or individual. Therefore, ISO 31000:2009 is not specific to any industry or sector.

In addition, the standards can be applied throughout the life of an organization, and to a wide range of activities, including strategies and decisions, operations, processes, functions, projects, products, services and assets.

ISO 31000: 2009 can be applied to any type of risk, whatever its nature, regardless of whether it has positive or negative consequences.[1]

BANK FOR INTERNATIONAL SETTLEMENT (BIS) AND BASEL COMMITTEE

Bank for International Settlement (BIS) is the world's oldest international financial institution, established in the year 1930, with headquarters in Basel, Switzerland.

The mission of BIS is to 'serve central banks in their pursuit of monetary and financial stability, to foster international cooperation in those areas and to act as a bank for central banks'.[2]

Of the various committees that BIS operates, the Basel Committee on Banking Supervision is the key international body that provides a forum for regular cooperation on banking supervisory matters. In 1988, the committee introduced a capital measurement system, commonly referred to as the Basel Capital Accord or (Basel I). The accord provided calculations for minimum risk–based capital adequacy for the banks, keeping it at a minimum of 8 per cent of the banks, risk weighted assets (RWA). RWA is a measure to quantify credit risk. To exemplify, let's suppose a bank has extended a loan of Rs 175 lakh to a variety of its customers (see Table 3.1). In addition, the bank has Rs 25 lakh as cash. To assess its credit risk, Basel I would require multiplying these loans and the cash level with the risk weights assigned to each category of loan. Since a risk weight of 50 per cent is given for home loans, a home loan of Rs 50 lakh would translate into $50 \times 0.5 = 25$ as an RWA. The sum of all RWAs would then be the total RWA for the bank.

As illustrated in Table 3.1, assets of the bank worth Rs 200 lakh translate into Rs 60 lakh of RWAs. Note that cash and government bonds are considered risk-free and hence have zero risk weight. For the Rs 60 lakh RWAs, the Basel Accord requires the bank to keep a minimum of 8 per cent as its own capital to cover the loss. So the bank should be keeping a minimum of Rs 4.8 lakh as capital.

While Basel I was a great breakthrough in terms of defining credit risk and how much capital banks should

TABLE 3.1: Illustration of Risk Weighted Assets

(All figures in Rs lakh)

Type of Asset	Monetary Value of Assets (A)	Risk Weight (B)	Risk Weighted Asset (A×B)
Cash	25	0%	0
Government Bond	50	0%	0
Municipal Bond	50	20%	10
Home Loan	50	50%	25
Credit Card Loan	25	100%	25
Total	**200**		**60**

keep to cover losses, it was too narrow in its scope. The biggest drawback of Basel I was that it provided only four broad categories of credit risk weights (0 per cent, 20 per cent, 50 per cent and 100 per cent), and it failed to cover other aspects of risk such as operational risk in calculating minimum capital requirement. To overcome all these drawbacks, Basel II was introduced in 2004.

Basel II

The framework for Basel II consists of three pillars, namely:

1. Minimum regulatory capital requirement
2. Supervisory review
3. Market discipline (disclosures)

FIGURE 3.2: The Three Pillars of Basel II

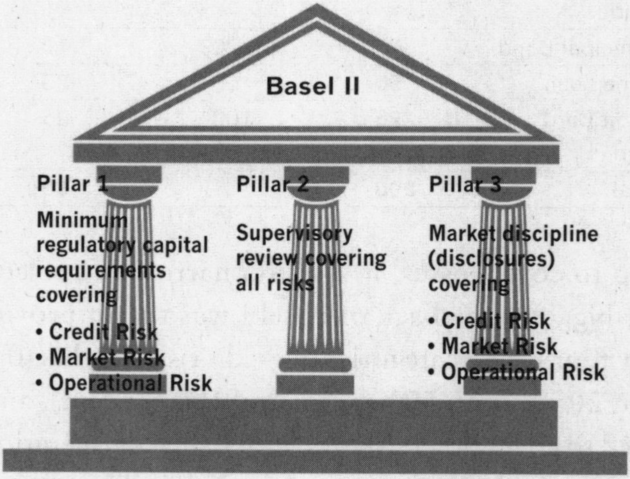

Basel II

Pillar 1
Minimum regulatory capital requirements covering
• Credit Risk
• Market Risk
• Operational Risk

Pillar 2
Supervisory review covering all risks

Pillar 3
Market discipline (disclosures) covering
• Credit Risk
• Market Risk
• Operational Risk

PILLAR I

The first pillar considers calculating minimum capital requirement for three types of financial risks: credit risk, market risk and operational risk.

For credit risk, Basel II introduces the internal risk-based (IRB) approach wherein financial institutions are allowed to use their own measures of credit risk for the purpose of calculating capital requirements. This approach serves as an alternative to the standardized approach of calculating RWAs as discussed above.

The basic components of credit risk that are estimated in IRB approaches are probability of default (PD), exposure at default (EAD) and loss given default (LGD). To illustrate, suppose a bank has given a credit card to a customer with a credit line of Rs 1,00,000. The bank estimates that in the next twenty-four months, there is a 20 per cent chance that the customer will not repay the loan. Hence, the probability of default (PD) is 20 per cent. Moreover, the bank has estimated that the customer will utilize 40 per cent of his line (Rs 40,000) when he defaults on the loan. This is called exposure at default (EAD). In addition, the bank has also calculated that it can recover 25 per cent of the amount at exposure by working with the customer through a new payment plan. So, loss given default (LGD) = 1 − Recovery Rate = 1 − 0.25 = 0.75. Hence, expected loss by the bank on this customer = PD × EAD × LGD = 0.2 × 40,000 × 0.75 = Rs 6000.

In the foundation IRB approach, the bank calculates the value of PD based on internal data and relies on EAD and LGD estimates to be provided by the regulator. In the advanced approach, all three components are computed internally by the bank.

FIGURE 3.3: Expected Loss

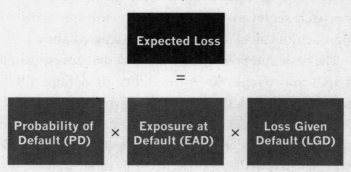

In addition to expected losses, one must also keep a note of the unexpected losses, or the losses that may exceed the expected level in any period due to rare events. One must be prepared for these events at all times as they have the highest chance of disrupting the business. A business should have adequate capital to cover not only the expected losses but unexpected ones as well.

The second type of risk, market risk, is measured by the value at risk (VaR) approach. VaR measures the threshold value below which the value of the portfolio will not fall with a given specified probability and within a specified time horizon. Two elements are critical to calculate VaR: specified probability and time horizon.

For example, if an investor has invested Rs 1,00,000

in the stock market then 95 per cent weekly VaR of Rs 10,000 signifies that over the next one week there is a 95 per cent chance that the value of the portfolio will not fall by more than 10,000 or, in other words, there is a 5 per cent chance that in the next one week the value will fall by more than 10,000.[3]

A third type of risk, operational risk, is measured by a variety of approaches, such as the standardized approach, basic indicator approach and advanced measurement approach.[4]

PILLAR 2: SUPERVISORY REVIEW

The second pillar requires supervisors/regulators to review the activities of the bank, assess their capital requirements and advise them to keep extra capital over and above the minimum regulatory capital, if required, and suggest any remedial actions.

PILLAR 3: MARKET DISCIPLINE

This pillar aims to provide transparency in a bank's activities so that market participants are able to gauge the efficacy of the management and the capital adequacy of that bank. This pillar complements the first two pillars and requires the institutions to disclose their practices to the public in order to foster a better governance system.

When market participants have a better understanding of risk management practices of banks and how banks use the funds at their disposal, participants can rank the institutions that are doing better than others and hence an element of market discipline sets in the system.

SUMMARY

Risk is omnipresent and omniscient. For decisions involving money, it is imperative to understand, assess and manage risk before money is invested, lest an investor lose all his/her wealth. This chapter discussed the concept of risk, its various types and some standard frameworks that financial institutions employ to manage financial risk.

The Basel Committee doesn't possess any supranational powers and hence its conclusions and recommendations are not legally binding on its member nations. However, its broad supervisory standards, guidelines and best practices provide a framework for the member institutions that adopt the practices in their best interest while working within the boundaries of national systems.

In October 1999, the RBI issued guidelines to Indian banks with clear expectations, integrating some of the international standards of risk management.

YOU MUST ALSO KNOW

➤ In response to the financial crisis of 2008, the Basel Committee has proposed a new set of global standards to address both firm-specific and broader system risk. These guidelines are referred to as Basel III. This requires banks to keep an additional cushion (beyond the level of Basel II) to cover losses.

➤ A theory of black swan events was developed by Nassim Nicholas Taleb to describe highly improbable events that have a huge impact for the participant. It was such events that played a key role in the unexpected losses during the sub-prime crisis of 2008. These events are very hard to predict, although in hindsight, they can be easily rationalized.

CHAPTER 4

PUTTING YOUR EGGS IN DIFFERENT BASKETS

Mr Srinivasan has been an avid investor in the stock market for quite a few years. Due to his interest in the financial sector and belief in the sector's performance, he has invested the majority of his funds in the stocks of major Indian banks. While he enjoyed considerable gains when the financial sector performed well, he lost almost all his investment when there was a meltdown in the global economy during the sub-prime crisis of 2008, which severely impacted the financial sector across the globe. Could Mr Srinivasan have done better by spreading his investments across sectors (automotive, health care, etc.) than by 'putting all his eggs in one basket'? Would that have required sacrificing some of the exorbitant returns he was enjoying in the financial sector?

All these questions lie at the heart of effective portfolio management. For an individual investor, a portfolio can be defined as a combination of stocks, bonds, mutual funds, fixed deposit or any other type of investment that she chooses to form a part of her investment plan. For corporations, a portfolio would comprise all the strategic projects that it has invested in; for financial institutions such as banks, a portfolio would include all the loans that a bank has extended to its customers. More broadly, a portfolio is a combination of different types of assets towards which an investment has been made. Portfolio management would then involve a series of steps required to create a portfolio and manage it over time with the objective of getting maximum returns at minimum risk.

PORTFOLIO RISK AND RETURN

In chapter 3, we defined the risk on any stand-alone investment as the variance of return during the period under consideration. For a portfolio of investments, the risk is not only related to the variance in individual investments, but also on the covariance between the investments. In simple terms, covariance signifies how two variables change together. If an investor has a portfolio of two stocks whose returns in an extreme condition are highly negatively related to each other, such that if the return on one falls below the expected value, the return on the other goes above the expected value and vice versa, the investor is hedged or covered against the loss of return if she invests in only one of the stocks. This is the benefit of diversification of investment or, in other words, putting your eggs in different baskets.

This approach of maximizing returns while minimizing risks by diversification was propounded by Harry Markowitz in the early 1960s and is widely recognized as modern portfolio theory.

For the interested reader, the detailed calculation of covariance and portfolio risk and return is shown in Example 4.1; however, Figure 4.1 provides a quick glance at the risk–return trade-off for a portfolio of two stocks, A and B, with varying degrees of investment in each.

Stock A is less risky and provides lower return than Stock B. Point 1 through Point 4 on the graph depicts an increasing percentage of investment in Stock B. For example, Point 1 depicts 100 per cent investment in

FIGURE 4.1: Risk–Return Trade-off for a Portfolio of
Two Stocks

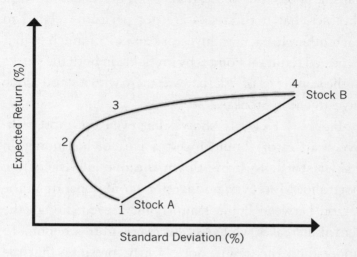

Stock A and 0 per cent in Stock B, while Point 3 may depict 70 per cent in Stock A and 30 per cent in Stock B. Point 4 shows 100 per cent investment in Stock B.[*]

A risk-averse investor would tend to choose Point 1 on the graph by investing 100 per cent in Stock A and be satisfied with the lower expected return. But is this the optimal point for a risk-free investor? Clearly not. As is evident from the graph, there is a backward bend in the overall portfolio standard deviation as the

[*] Point 3 is vertically above Point 1 on the graph.

investor chooses to increase the investment in Stock B. This happens due to the gains from diversification and the fact that both stocks are not perfectly related to each other. In fact, an investor can gain a much higher expected return at Point 3 by investing in both the stocks at the same level of risk that was there with a stand-alone investment in Stock A.

Figure 4.1 clearly shows that even the most risk-averse investor should invest a part of his money in riskier stock, to bring down the overall risk of the portfolio. Moreover, no investor should operate in the region between Point 1 and Point 2 even though the return increases while risk decreases in this region. To understand this point more clearly, presume that the investor chooses a point X between Point 1 and Point 2. If you draw a vertical line passing through point X, you see that the line cuts the curve again at a point Y between Point 2 and Point 3. The portfolio Y has the same risk as portfolio X while it has a higher return than portfolio X. Hence, for the investor portfolio Y is a better choice than portfolio X, and any rational investor would not operate between Point 1 and Point 2.

The optimal point for most risk-averse investors would be Point 2, while for others the actual point between Point 2 and Point 4 would depend upon their risk preference. The segment between Point 2 and Point 4 is generally referred to as the 'efficient frontier' because it provides the best combination of risk and return for a given allocation of investment between two stocks.

The red line can be compared against the base scenario (blue line) when two stocks are perfectly correlated with each other. In this case, there are no gains from diversification and the straight line between Point 1 and Point 4 depicts the risk–return trade-off. Hence, compared to the base case, the lower the correlation between the movements of the two stocks, the greater the backward bend of the trade-off line will be, and so, the benefits would be higher due to diversification.

PORTFOLIO RISK AND RETURN IN THE PRESENCE OF A RISK-FREE ASSET

So far we have looked at creating a portfolio of two risky stocks, A and B. What if we introduce a risk-free asset in the choice set such as a fixed deposit or government bond?

Figure 4.2 highlights such an asset with expected return Rf and standard deviation of 0. So the asset would lie on the Y axis with return = Rf.

Now an investor has a choice of combining the

risk-free asset with a choice of risky assets. Even the most risk-averse investor, who would choose Point 2 on the efficient frontier as the optimal combination of Stock A and Stock B, can do better by allocating a part of her money to a risk-free asset and portfolio M of risky assets. By doing so, she would gain much higher expected return (at Point 2), while maintaining the same amount of risk as at Point 2.

Thus portfolio M turns out to be the preferred and optimal portfolio for any investor. An investor can either hold this portfolio M by investing all the money in it, or she can combine it with a risk-free asset by investing a portion of money in the latter. In either case, an investor's choice of portfolio would lie on the green line, a tangent to the efficient frontier passing through Rf.

Portfolio M is referred to as the 'market portfolio' or a portfolio that represents the market such as the SENSEX.

For gains from diversification, we need not necessarily require negatively correlated stocks. As long as the correlation is less than 1, diversification will yield results.

FIGURE 4.2: Risk–Return Trade-off for a Portfolio of Two Stocks in the Presence of a Risk-Free Asset

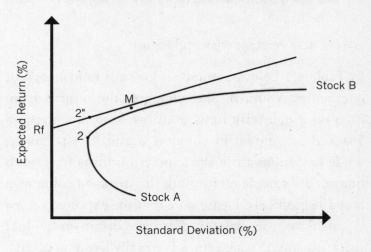

The concept of the efficient frontier can be extended to multiple stocks in the portfolio and also to the combination of portfolios themselves. However, as the number of stocks in the portfolio increases, the calculation of standard deviation of the portfolio becomes quite tedious. This is due to the number of covariance terms that need to be calculated between pairs of stocks.

For a reader interested in numbers and calculations, the following example attempts to explain the concept.

EXAMPLE 4.1: Portfolio Risk and Return

In Table 4.1 below, assume an investor holds stock of companies A and B. She compares the returns from each on a quarterly basis. Returns from Stock A and Stock B are shown in columns 2 and 4 respectively, while deviations from the expected returns from each quarter are calculated for both the stocks in columns 3 and 5 respectively. Please note that the expected return is calculated by averaging returns on an individual stock (assuming each return is equally likely to occur). So, the average of column 2 gives an expected return on Stock A = 0.125 and the average of column 3 will give an expected return on Stock B = 0.05. Assume that an investor allocates 50 per cent of her investment to Stock A and the remaining 50 per cent to Stock B, the expected return on the portfolio would be the weighted average of the returns on each stock, weights being the percentage of the amount of money invested in each. So, *expected return on the portfolio* = 0.5 × 0.125 + 0.5 × 0.05 = 0.0875.

TABLE 4.1: Expected Return on the Portfolio

	Return on Stock A	Deviation from Expected Return (=0.125)	Return on Stock B	Deviation from Expected Return (=0.05)	Product of Deviations
Quarter 1	0.3	0.175	-0.2	-0.25	-0.04375
Quarter 2	-0.2	-0.325	0.1	0.05	-0.01625
Quarter 3	0.5	0.375	-0.3	-0.35	-0.13125
Quarter 4	-0.1	-0.225	0.6	0.55	-0.12375

What about the expected risk of the portfolio? We know that the individual standard deviations of Stock A and Stock B are 0.286 and 0.35 respectively. Would the expected standard deviation of the portfolio be the weighted average of the standard deviation of the two stocks, that is, $0.5 \times 0.286 + 0.5 \times 0.35 = 0.318$? Well, the answer is No.

The risk of the portfolio depends not only on the individual variances of the stocks comprising the portfolio but also on the covariance between the set of stocks. The general formula for the risk of the portfolio comprising two stocks is given as

Variance (portfolio) = $Wa^2 \times \sigma a^2 + Wb^2 \times \sigma b^2 + 2Wa \times Wb \times$ Covariance (A,B)

where *Wa* and *Wb* are the percentages of investment in Stock A and Stock B respectively, and σa and σb are the standard deviations of the two stocks.

Please note that a positive covariance between the two stocks enhances the portfolio variance of the portfolio while negative covariance reduces the same.

For our example, we will start by calculating the covariance between the two stocks. For that we need to calculate the deviation of the stocks' returns from the expected value. The same is done in columns 3 and 5 for each of the stocks. Covariance is then calculated by taking a product of two deviations (in column 6) and then taking an average of these. So, covariance for Stock A and Stock B turns out to be −0.0785. Here, covariance has a negative sign, implying that when one stock's return is below average, the other stock's return is likely to be above its average.

Variance of our portfolio = $0.5^2 \times 0.286^2 + 0.5^2 \times 0.35^2$
$+ 2 \times 0.5 \times 0.5 \times -0.0785 = 0.0117$

Since standard deviation is equal to the square root of variance, in our example standard deviation turns out to be $\sqrt{(0.0117)} = 0.1082$. This value is less than the weighted average standard deviation of 0.318 as calculated before.

A related concept of correlation also needs to be mentioned here. Since the magnitude of covariance (0.0785 in the example above) is hard to interpret, a related concept of correlation is used. Correlation is calculated by dividing the covariance by the standard deviation of each of the stocks. The correlation coefficient always lies between −1 and +1. While −1 implies that the two variables in question are perfectly negatively correlated, +1 refers to a strong positive correlation between them.[1]

Correlation (ρ) = Covariance(A,B)/$(\sigma a \times \sigma b)$

We can rewrite our portfolio variance of a two-asset formula in terms of the correlation coefficient as follows:

Variance = $Wa^2 \times \sigma a^2 + Wb^2 \times \sigma b^2 + 2Wa \times Wb \times \sigma a \times \sigma b \times \rho$

where ρ is the correlation coefficient

In the extreme case of the correlation coefficient being 1, portfolio variance would equal the weighted standard deviation of a portfolio. This would refer to the case of a straight line between Point 1 and Point 4 in Figure 4.1. So as long as the correlation is less than 1, there are gains in risk by diversifying the portfolio to include more stocks.

In the case of a portfolio having N assets with an equal amount invested in each of them, the portfolio risk can be written as

Variance (portfolio of N assets) =
$\frac{1}{N} \times$ Average Variance $+ \left(1 - \frac{1}{N}\right) \times$ Average Covariance

The general equation implies that as the numbers of assets/stocks in the portfolio increases, the average covariance between assets plays a greater role in defining the risk of the portfolio than individual variances. This can be seen from the equation as the first term (average variance/N) tends towards zero as N becomes large.

Also, the second term would tend towards average covariance as the number of assets increases. This implies that the risk of the portfolio can never become zero (unless average covariance equals zero). This risk is called non-diversifiable or market risk and would continue to exist even with diversification. In our example at the opening of this chapter, Mr Srinivasan may diversify and eliminate some of the risk by adding health-care stocks to his existing portfolio of bank stocks, but he would continue to be exposed to market risk that would impact all the stocks in general.

FIGURE 4.3: Unique Risks versus Market Risks

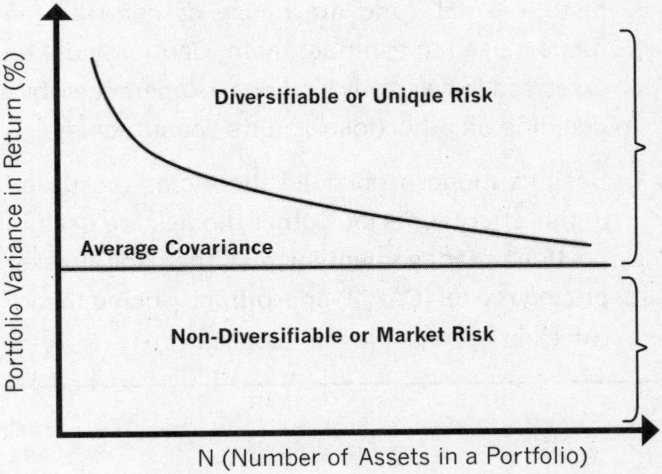

Diversifiable or Unique Risk

Average Covariance

Non-Diversifiable or Market Risk

Portfolio Variance in Return (%)

N (Number of Assets in a Portfolio)

SUMMARY

Portfolio management is critical to any investor or financial institution having assets or investments across different products. There are clear gains that one can derive by effectively managing the portfolio. This chapter attempted to explain this by touching upon the modern portfolio theory and its constituents.

YOU MUST ALSO KNOW

➢ Expected returns on a portfolio are based on historical data and are hence as good as the models used to estimate them. Caution must be exercised to avoid any irrational exuberance while deciding on a portfolio and its constituents.

➢ Besides modern portfolio theory, as discussed in this chapter, various other models are used in portfolio management such as the capital asset pricing model (CAPM) or arbitrage pricing theory (APT).[2]

CHAPTER 5

ASSESSING A CUSTOMER'S VALUE

The marketing division plays a very significant role in any business. While at the front end, it serves as an important interface to the customers, behind the scenes it takes decisions that propel the business forward. These decisions include but are not limited to (a) identification of valuable customers, (b) acquisition of new customers, (c) impact of new sales activities and (d) customer retention. In this chapter on marketing analytics we shall explore how analytical tools are leveraged to improve marketing decisions.

Bala has recently joined as chief of marketing in a B2B (business-to-business) company. At his earlier workplace, Bala looked after the customer relationship management (CRM) function. He is thus conversant with the different marketing analytics and metrics that are frequently used for making and evaluating marketing decisions. One of the key tasks that Bala is expected to carry out immediately after joining is to identify those customers who matter most to the company. These are the customers who bring maximum value to the company and need to be retained. Also, while acquiring new customers it is desirable that only those customers who could add substantial value to the company be acquired. Thus, identifying 'valuable' customers is one of the most important tasks before marketing heads like Bala.

CUSTOMER LIFETIME VALUE

To solve his problem, Bala can turn to the concept of customer lifetime value (CLV). The concept is quite powerful and is used by many businesses around the world. For example, in the hospitality sector CLV can be used to offer free room upgrades, while in the airlines industry it can be used to offer discounted fares to the customers with high value. In general, knowing the value of the customer is probably one of the key things that any marketing manager would aspire for because this can be leveraged to not only offer discounted products, superior customer service and loyalty programmes, it can also act as an early warning system when customers start to engage less and hence corrective action is required.

To identify valuable customers it is important to have an estimate of the lifetime value of a customer. Customers with a high lifetime value need to be engaged in a different manner from those with a low lifetime value. In principle, CLV is easy to state. It is the net margin per sales multiplied by the number of sales that can be made to the customer over his entire lifetime minus the acquisition cost for that customer, all suitably adjusted to present value terms.

Simplified Formula to Calculate Customer Lifetime Value

Assume customer stays with the company for t years

$CLV =$ in year 1

   (Net Margin per Sale × Number of Sales)$/(1+r)$

   +

   (Net Margin per Sale × Number of Sales)$/(1+r)^2$ in year 2

   +

   (Net Margin per Sale × Number of Sales)$/(1+r)^3$ in year 3

   −

   Cost of acquiring the customer

where r is the appropriate discount factor to calculate Net Present Value and

   Net Margin per Sale = Revenue from Sale − Cost of Sale

Though the definition is simple it involves considerable challenges in estimation.

Firstly, in non-contractual settings, the number of sales that can be made to a customer over his entire lifetime is difficult to estimate as the customer has the freedom to switch to a different company/brand at any point of time, a phenomenon captured through a metric called retention rate. To exemplify, suppose a new mobile service provider acquires 1000 new customers during a particular year. Of the 1000 customers, suppose 800 like the service and hence remain with the service provider the next year; here, the retention rate is 80 per cent. One can interpret this number to mean that on average there is an 80 per cent chance of any new customer acquired during a particular year staying with the company. However, the retention rate may vary over time. For example, of the 800 customers in the second year, if 720 stay on for the third year, the retention rate for the third year turns out to be 90 per cent. In general, the retention rate improves over time as only the loyal customers remain with a company.

Secondly, the simplifying assumption that the net margin per sale is the same for all sales made during a customer's lifetime is often unrealistic and may need suitable modification.

Finally, since the time of a sale is not deterministic the present value of the cash flows becomes a random variable.

FIGURE 5.1: Three Critical Elements for Customer Lifetime Calculation

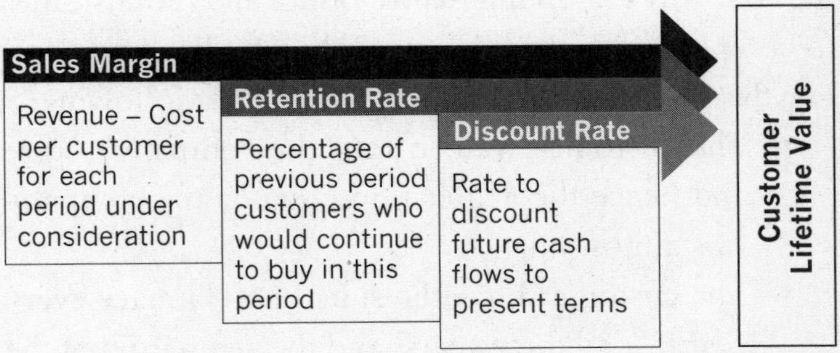

Care must be taken in estimating the retention rate of customers who often repeat purchase after a long period of inactivity. One may wrongly assume a customer to be lost for good and hence estimate a lower value, while the customer may simply come back after some time. This scenario is quite prevalent in big-ticket purchases such as electronic goods.

CLV CALCULATIONS: SOME SIMPLE SCENARIOS

In the following examples, we will set aside the complications mentioned above and try to compute the customer lifetime value for a few simple situations. We will restrict ourselves to a three-year horizon and assume the company to be a high-end clothier and the customer to be a professional who loves to shop for business suits. For the sake of simplicity, let's assume the following:

- The customer walked into the company's store and hence the acquisition cost for the company was almost nil.
- The customer buys the suits on 1 January every year (for all three years) and the net margin of the company per sale of this product is Rs 1000.
- A discount rate of 10 per cent per annum.

The CLV for this customer (in rupees) is then

$$\frac{1000}{(1+0.1)} + \frac{1000}{(1+0.1)^2} + \frac{1000}{(1+0.1)^3} = 2486.85$$

This CLV number has a lot of significance for the company. If the company were to calculate this number for all the customers, it would come to know which customers are more valuable than others, and hence it can offer higher discounts to the high-valued customers. Another usage is that if the company were to spend money to acquire this customer, this value would be the maximum it can afford to spend, otherwise the net lifetime profit for the company from this customer would be negative.

The time horizon considered for calculating CLV may play a critical role in the final estimate of a customer's value. In some scenarios and industries, which use infinite horizon to calculate CLV, a customer may be of double the value over an infinite horizon compared to the value over a three- to five-year horizon. In practice, one should choose a time horizon for a customer where retention rate becomes insignificant or where sales are negligible for an average customer.

In the above scenario, we have assumed that the customer will continue to buy the business suits for three years with certainty. In reality, this will not happen as it is possible for the customer to switch to a different company or brand. We now modify the above example by taking this fact into account. We assume that the chance that the customer buys the suit in the first year is 0.8, in the second year is 0.64 and in the third year is 0.512. To compute the expected CLV we would now take the expected cash flows into account for the uncertainty regarding the customer's purchase of the product. The expected cash flows are computed by multiplying the net margin from a sale with the probability of making that sale. Thus, we get the expected CLV (in rupees) as

$$\frac{(1000 \times 0.8)}{(1 + 0.1)} + \frac{(1000 \times 0.64)}{(1 + 0.1)^2} + \frac{(1000 \times 0.512)}{(1 + 0.1)^3} = 1640.87$$

By comparing the two figures given in the above two paragraphs it is easy to see that the expected CLV is strongly dependent on the probability of purchase. It is therefore worthwhile for a marketing manager to invest resources to increase the probability of purchase of this product over the specified time horizon. Let us suppose that a marketing manager has decided to give discounts for the purchase of business suits in the second and third years. He will give a discount of 10 per cent if the suit is bought in the second year and 20 per cent if the suit is bought in the third year. Through this exercise he wants to increase the purchase probability for the second year to 0.72 from the present 0.64 and for the third year to 0.65 from the present 0.512. A question of interest is whether this scheme is worthwhile for the company. This scheme will be worthwhile for this company if the CLV increases from the present Rs 1640.87. We calculate the expected CLV under this scheme as

$$\frac{(1000 \times 0.8)}{1.1} + \frac{(900 \times 0.72)}{1.1^2} + \frac{(800 \times 0.65)}{1.1^3} = 1653.49$$

Thus, we see that the discount scheme enhances the CLV, although marginally, and hence should be offered to the customer.

SUMMARY

CLV is a powerful tool that businesses can leverage to assess the value of their customers. The same can be used to either offer loyalty programmes, discount schemes or cross-sell offers to the high-valued customers. In addition, this can generate insights into customers who are less engaged with the business and whether there is any value in taking remedial action. So much power in just this one number—CLV.

Back-of-the-Envelope CLV Calculation

CLV = (Revenue – Cost for a period)/Discount rate

The formula assumes:

1. Constant sales margin over periods
2. Infinite time horizon
3. 100 per cent retention rate for a customer
4. Cash flow at the end of the period

YOU MUST ALSO KNOW

➤ While the CLV model takes a futuristic view to identify profitable customers, there are also frameworks that evaluate past behaviour to identify profitable segments. One such popular framework is based on the recency of purchase, frequency of purchase and monetary value of past purchase, in short called the RFM framework.

➤ One can improve the predictive power of a simple CLV framework by developing sophisticated models to estimate customers' survival rate at various points of time, by predicting the varying purchase behaviour during and across the periods and by incorporating referrals by existing customers to which a programme is targeted.

CHAPTER 6

SEGMENTING THE MARKET

Geet's company is planning to introduce a new product in the market. The company has been in the consulting field for a long time but has little experience in product marketing. The new product aims to meet the requirements of a business manager to convert a document into a format for presentation. The company came up with this product after market research indicated that many managers have difficulty in making presentations based on documents made by others. One of the challenges faced was that the documents came in various forms—some printed, some in soft-copy form as Word documents or PDFs, handwritten notes, etc. Since business managers are a large class, Geet felt the need to divide them into smaller classes so that effective marketing promotion strategies could be devised for them. Geet could easily see that not all business managers needed this product; for example, those primarily handling operations in manufacturing organizations do not make presentations often, and so, would not need this product. But marketing and finance managers may view this product favourably as they are often asked to make presentations both within and outside the company. Also, general managers and chief executives would find this product helpful as they are hard-pressed for time and need to bring in data from many sources of information while making a presentation. This product may also reduce their dependence on subordinates. These different categories of managers need to be addressed separately for the promotion of this product and hence Geet is required to use the techniques of market segmentation to achieve the objectives.

SEGMENTATION TECHNIQUES

Segmentation is a technical term used for dividing a heterogeneous group of potential customers into several homogeneous groups. The homogeneity may be in terms of their needs, demographic profile, socio-economic characteristics, etc. In marketing, segmentation is generally followed by targeting, wherein a business selects the specific segments to be targeted for its product. A business can then develop detailed product positioning in the specific targeted segments. This framework is commonly referred to as STP—segmentation, targeting and positioning—in marketing parlance. For Geet, the finance and marketing managers formed one segment while the general managers and chief executives formed another segment.

There are various statistical methods to create market segments; however, the most commonly used is called clustering. In clustering, the characteristics of the potential customers are used to identify groups that are homogeneous. Once the clusters are formed, the manager can think of devising communication or targeting strategies to reach these potential customers.

Geet decided to collect information from various managers on these bases: (a) the average number of presentations made by them in a month, (b) the average number of slides in a presentation, (c) the average number of sources of information that they needed to consult to make a presentation and (d) the average time taken to make a presentation. He thought of collecting this information through a survey conducted by a reputed market research agency. To get an accurate

FIGURE 6.1: Clustering of Objects Based on
Colour and Shape

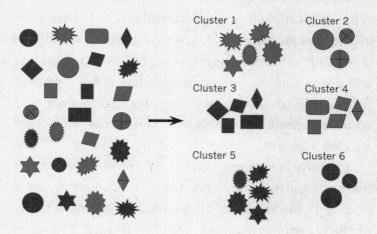

picture he decided to advise the agency to follow a panel data approach whereby the managers would be queried every week regarding these four criteria. While this was a costly approach, Geet thought that it would ensure good data quality as it would be largely free from recollection errors. Subsequent to getting these data, Geet planned to advise the analysis team in his organization to run a cluster analysis. While Geet had no clear idea about the exact number of clusters, he could guess that it would be somewhere between four and six. He therefore intended to suggest to the analysis team that all three solutions, namely, those with four clusters, five clusters and six clusters, be investigated and the one with the best business interpretation be chosen for further action.

AN OVERVIEW OF THE CLUSTERING PROCESS

Geet's analysis team collected the required information through a survey targeted at 1000 companies spread across India. The analysts were then ready to perform a cluster analysis with the data at hand, with an objective to group companies that were as similar as possible compared with the companies within the same cluster and as dissimilar as possible when compared with the companies in another cluster.

Clustering analysis, broadly, can be described as a three-stage process as highlighted in Figure 6.2.

The first stage requires partitioning of the dataset and involves a decision on the following key elements of the process:

a) **How to measure the similarity/dissimilarity between clusters.**
   To measure whether two observations (or clusters) are similar to each other, a variety of measures can

FIGURE 6.2: An Overview of the Clustering Process

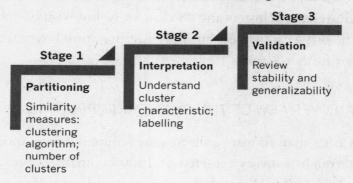

be deployed, such as distance, correlation, etc. Geet's team used a simple Euclidean distance measure to find the similarity between the observations.

Euclidean distance is a straight-line distance between two observations calculated as

$$D_{ij} = \sqrt{\sum_{k=1}^{n} (x_{ki} - x_{kj})^2}$$

for observations i and j.

b) **What algorithm should be used to cluster the observations?**

The next big challenge for Geet's team was to decide the way in which to proceed for clustering the observations. There are various techniques available to carry out the grouping, such as hierarchical clustering, where one can start with N clusters and start grouping them until it reaches 1 cluster, or one can start with 1 big cluster of an entire dataset and keep splitting till it reaches N clusters. Among the non-hierarchical clustering methods, the k-means clustering is the most popular. This method works well if the customer's characteristics are mostly numeric variables. Most software packages have a routine for performing k-means clustering. One of the key issues in k-means clustering is the choice of k, which is the number of clusters to be formed. Often, k is determined from the information available in the application context. In cases where no such information is available, k can be determined through statistical means.

c) **How many clusters should be created?**

The number of clusters, theoretically, can lie between 1 and N, where N is the number of records in the dataset. At the extreme, a 1 cluster solution will not provide any value as this would amount to looking at the entire dataset together and clubbing it into one segment, thus providing no additional information. On the other extreme, the N cluster solution is also not useful as it amounts to looking at each observation individually without any aggregation. Thus, the optimal number of clusters should lie between the extremes.

In the hierarchical method of clustering, the similarity of observations dilutes if we keep adding dissimilar observations to a cluster. The optimal number of clusters would be the point where the dissimilarity increases remarkably for a small decrease in the number of clusters. This is highlighted in Figure 6.3.

FIGURE 6.3: Optimal Number of Clusters

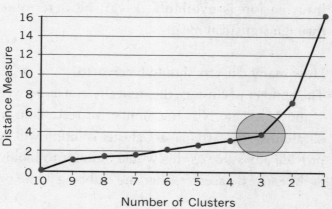

Based on the analysis, Geet's team decide to keep three clusters in the final proposal.

The second stage of clustering entails the interpretation of the generated clusters and labelling them appropriately based on the cluster characteristics so that effective targeting can be done for each.

TABLE 6.1: Cluster Interpretation and Labelling

Dimension	Cluster 1	Cluster 2	Cluster 3
Average number of monthly presentations	5	35	15
Average number of slides in a presentation	7	15	25
Average time taken to make a presentation (in hours)	1.4	2.5	4.5
Average number of sources required to make a presentation	3	5	4
Percentage of total population in a cluster	35%	40%	25%
LABEL	Self-sufficient	Low-hanging fruits	Full steam ahead

After analysing the cluster information in Table 6.1, it is evident that Cluster 1 creates the lowest number of presentations, having the fewest slides per month, compared to the other clusters. Cluster 2 creates the maximum number of presentations, though the average number of slides is lower than Cluster 3. Cluster 3, due to its large number of slides per presentation, takes the maximum time to create one presentation.

Based on this data, Geet's team recommends targeting Cluster 2 and Cluster 3 for the potential sale of his company's new product that assists in making presentations. These clusters are more likely to use this product than Cluster 1. By targeting Cluster 2 and Cluster 3, Geet would be targeting around 65 per cent (40 per cent in Cluster 2 and 25 per cent in Cluster 3) of the total potential market available for the product. The team has also labelled the clusters based on their characteristics and likelihood of using the product.

The final stage, stage three, of the clustering process required Geet's team to ensure that the results from the process are generalizable and hence can be applied to the overall population. In order to proceed with this stage, the analysts could either look at another data sample and validate the clustering results from it or they could subdivide the original 1000 records into two random samples and use one for clustering and the other for validation of the results from the clustering.

Geet has finally decided to send the product promotion offers to two of the identified clusters. He expects a favourable response—at least 40 per cent—from each of the clusters and waits anxiously for the promotion results to be seen in the next couple of months.

The clustering solution is as good as the number and type of variables used in the analysis. Care must be taken in selecting or deleting the characteristics from the analysis. The clustering technique, by itself, has no means to suggest if any characteristic is significant or not.

Please note that for good and stable results, the clustering technique requires close attention to factors such as outliers (objects having extreme characteristics), standardization of data (characteristics having different scales) and multicollinearity (high correlation among characteristics).

The clustering technique should be used only for descriptive/exploratory purposes. Since there is no statistical basis that can be used to draw inferences from sample to population, using the technique for inferential purposes may yield poor results.

YOU MUST ALSO KNOW

➢ The clustering technique has a broad range of applications from the field of psychology (grouping individuals based on personality characteristics) to the field of medicine, social sciences, market research and others.

➢ Cluster analysis is one of the ways of classifying objects/people. The other well-known methods are CHAID (Chi-square Automatic Interaction Detection) and CART (Classification and Regression Tree). However, these methods, unlike clustering, require a dependent variable for segmentation.

CHAPTER 7

PREDICTIVE MODELLING

In the previous chapter, we learnt how Geet used the clustering technique to segment and group the potential customers for his new commercial product. A subset of these groups was to be targeted for the promotion of the product. Geet had identified three clusters and finally decided to send the product promotion offers to two of them. He expected a favourable response, at least 40 per cent, from each of the clusters.

Today, two months have passed since he rolled out the promotion. Besides sending mails to the targeted clusters, he also invested in Internet advertisements and special events to market the product. He is very enthusiastic about having introduced a unique product in the market. As he nervously reviews the results of his strategy, he finds that while the overall campaign has yielded positive results, the response rate is not up to his expectations. Only 15 per cent of the businesses have responded to the promotions. Geet feels that he could have saved a lot of money on promotion and mailing if he had the means to know who among his potential customers were most likely to respond. Then, instead of mailing the promotional offer to the entire cluster, he could have mailed it only to a part of the cluster. He wonders if he can learn from the results of this campaign and use them in the upcoming campaign for the same product, targeting similar clusters of a population that was left out of the previous campaign.

He calls up a friend who works in the analytics modelling division of a leading retail store in India and learns that he can improve upon his marketing results by either using a statistical regression technique (such as logistic regression) or with the help of data mining through decision trees (such as CHAID). Both the techniques are classified under predictive modelling. The following sections elaborate each of these methods and their applications.

LOGISTIC REGRESSION

Logistic regression is a statistical technique used to

predict the probability of the occurrence of any event. The event is binary in nature and assumes only two discrete values in a 'Yes/No' form such as success or failure in a project, payment or default on a personal loan, and so on.[1]

FIGURE 7.1: Some Examples of Binary Events

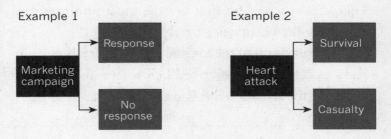

Non-binary event: more than two outcomes

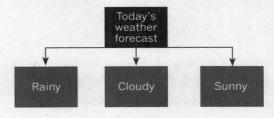

The event is captured in a dependent (or response) variable as either 0 or 1. Such variables, which take only two values, are known as indicator variables as they indicate the occurrence or non-occurrence of an event. In

Geet's case, this would translate into coding all targeted businesses that responded as 1 and those that did not as 0. The predicted values from logistic regression for each of the businesses would lie between 0 and 1 and hence can be considered as the probability/likelihood of responding to a campaign. The predictions would be based on certain variables, known as independent (or explanatory) variables that are the most important in explaining the occurrence of the event.

The application of the logistic regression technique in Geet's case has been described below (see also the box below for the logistic regression equation).

Logistic Regression

An equation of the following form is used for the dataset

$Logit(p) = a + b_1x_1 + b_2x_2 + \ldots + b_nx_n$

where

   $Logit(p)$ is defined as log (with natural base) of $p/1 - p$ where p is the probability of response = 1

   $x_1, x_2 \ldots x_n$ are the independent variables and

   $b_1, b_2 \ldots b_n$ are the respective coefficients as determined by the regression

Once the Logit(p) is calculated through the equation, one can derive the required probability using the transformation

$P = exp(Logit(p)) / (1 + exp(Logit(p)))$

Geet's team starts to work on the data from the last marketing campaign on their commercial product. The data contains 1000 targeted businesses with information on demographics, firmographics (number of employees, revenue, type of business, etc.), cluster tag (created during clustering), usage characteristics (number of monthly presentations, number of slides in each presentation, average time taken to prepare a presentation, etc.) for each of the business units. This set of information is known as independent (or explanatory) variables.

Geet's team has also created a dependent (or response) variable, capturing the businesses that responded as 1, and those who did not as 0. The percentage of responders in the dataset is 15 per cent.

The team uses the logistic regression technique to predict the probability of response for each of the businesses. Some of the significant variables in predicting response were total revenue of the business and usage characteristics (see above). Businesses having higher values for any of these variables had, on average, higher chances of responding to the campaign than the others, keeping everything else the same. The logistic regression results are summarized in the equation

Log $(p/1 - p) = -0.915 + 0.098 \times$ Total Revenue $+ 0.045$ $\times$ Number of Slides $+ 0.21 \times$ Average Time taken to prepare a presentation

where p is the probability of response

Using this equation, one can calculate the value of p for each of the observations (businesses).

As a final output of the logistic regression, the team gets the predicted probability for each of the businesses as highlighted in Table 7.1.

TABLE 7.1: Logistic Regression Output for a Sample of Observations

Observation (business)	Total revenue (in Rs million)	No. of slides in a presentation (in hours)	Avg. time taken to make a presentation (in hours)	Log(p/1–p) derived using regression equation	P (probability of response)
1	2	10	2	0.151	0.139
2	4	22	1	0.677	0.035
3	2	11	3	0.406	0.179
4	1	35	2	1.178	0.873
5	7	33	4	2.096	0.007

The next task is to choose the probability cut-off so that anyone above that value would be considered a potential responder and hence will be sent an offer in the next campaign. Any business whose probability value is below the chosen cut-off would be considered a non-responder and hence would be ignored in the next campaign.

Translating this into a decision rule:

Let p be the probability value for a particular business generated out of logistic regression and c be the chosen probability cut-off, then,

if p >= c, predicted response = Yes

if p < c, predicted response = No

This decision rule, however, leads to two kinds of misclassification errors as highlighted in Figure 7.2.

In Figure 7.2, blocks 1 and 4 have the correct classification while blocks 2 and 3 misclassify the businesses in terms of their response.

We can depict the quality of our decision through four key rates derived out of the classification matrix:

1. True Negative Rate = #4 / (#2 + #4)
2. False Positive Rate = #2 / (#2 + #4)
3. True Positive Rate = #1 / (#1 + #3)
4. False Negative Rate = #3 / (#1 + #3)

FIGURE 7.2: Classification Matrix

	Actual Response = Yes	Actual Response = No
Predicted Response = Yes	1 ✓	2 ✗
Predicted Response = No	3 ✗	4 ✓

These rates depend greatly on the chosen probability cut-off, c, used in the decision rule. If one chooses a low value of c, say close to zero, then all the businesses will be predicted to have Response = Yes. This will yield a very high True Positive Rate, but at the cost of a very low True Negative (or a high False Positive) Rate. On the contrary, if one chooses a high probability as cut-off, say close to 1, then all businesses would be considered to have a Response = No. This would result in a very high True Negative Rate, at the cost of a low True Positive Rate.

This then presents a dilemma before the decision maker as to what cut-off should be chosen. In many scenarios, the choice of cut-off depends upon the business objectives and the cost of making each type of error. One may choose to maximize both True Positive Rate and True Negative Rate while another may choose to focus on just minimizing the False Negative Rate.

Going back to our example, Geet's team decides to optimize the False Positive Rate and hence chooses the high cut-off value of c = 0.7. It does not want to spend money in sending offers to businesses that may appear to be responding but in fact will not.

Now, with the given logic to calculate the predicted probabilities of response and the optimal probability cut-off point, Geet's team is ready to use the logic on the potential businesses that can be targeted in the upcoming campaign. He can now save on the mailing costs and improve the profitability of his marketing campaign.

The following two equations hold in any scenario:

True Negative Rate + False Positive Rate = 1

True Positive Rate + False Negative Rate = 1

Work it out for yourself and see how it holds.

DECISION TREE: CHAID

As the word suggests, a decision tree produces a tree-like structure of decisions and hence assists in visualizing the possible scenarios with their consequences. In other words, it is a way of representing an algorithm or thought process in graphical format for better decision-making.

The acronym CHAID stands for Chi-square Automatic Interaction Detection. It derives its name from the Chi-square test of significance that is used as an algorithm to segment a sample based on various independent variables.[2]

In its basic form, CHAID attempts to establish a relationship between a dependent variable such as the popularity of a TV show and other independent variables, such as the length of the show, the star-cast, show timings, etc. CHAID then splits the sample under consideration into various segments that are as homogenous as possible within themselves and as heterogeneous as possible when compared across segments with respect to the dependent variable. The split is based on the most significant independent variables that differentiate the segments with respect to the dependent variable. The split happens in various steps with the first split picking the most significant variable and the next split the next best one, and so on. The splitting continues until the number of records in a segment is too low to split further or when the decision maker feels that the number of segments is optimal. The process produces a tree-like structure as depicted in Figure 7.3.

The application of the technique in Geet's case would make this technique clearer.

FIGURE 7.3: A Decision Tree

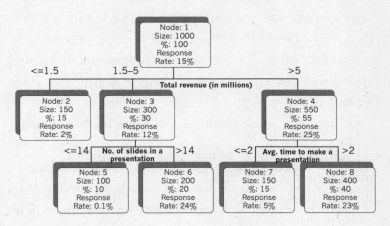

Geet's team uses the CHAID analysis on the data from the last-run marketing campaign. Its objective is to find the segments that differ with respect to the response rate to the last marketing offer.

In Figure 7.3, Node 1 is the starting point and

captures all the observations (size = 1000) from the last marketing offer. Node 1 is also called the parent node. The response rate of 15 per cent is highlighted in the node and represents the target variable that will be segmented in the process.

The tree uses total revenue as its first independent variable to split the population. This split produces three 'child nodes' with varying degrees of response rate. Node 2 with total revenue <= 1.5 million has around 15 per cent of total observations with a response rate = 2 per cent, while Node 4 has 55 per cent of observations with a response rate = 25 per cent. Note how the first-level split produces segments with response rates varying from 2 per cent to 25 per cent.

At the next level, Nodes 3 and 4 are further split by number of slides in a presentation and average time taken to make a presentation, respectively producing Nodes 5 to 7 in the process. Here again, the level of separation increases with Node 5 having the worst response rate of 0.1 per cent and Node 6 having the best response rate at 24 per cent.

Also note that Node 2 was not broken down further from level 1 as the response rate was too low. The team had already decided to reject this node from targeting in the next offer.

The final nodes in the tree, then, are Nodes 5, 6, 7 and 8. Out of these, Nodes 5 and 7 will be removed from the next mailing due to the poor response rate in the last mailing. Nodes 6 and 8 have healthy response rates and can be split further by other independent variables to improve the results.

Through the segmentation laid out in Figure 7.3, the team is able to identify 40 per cent of the targeted businesses which had the overall response rate of 2.7 per cent, and the remaining 60 per cent that had the response rate level of 23.7 per cent. Figure 7.4 highlights the details.

FIGURE 7.4: The Decision Nodes from the CHAID Analysis

	No. of observations	Response rate	Decision
Node 2	150	2%	REJECT (for the next mailing) No. of observations = 400 (40%) Response rate = 2.7%
Node 5	100	0.1%	
Node 7	150	5%	
Node 6	200	24%	ACCEPT (for the next mailing) No. of observations = 600 (60%) Response rate = 23.67%
Node 8	400	23%	

Geet's team is now equipped with two methods through which they can segment the businesses and improve the response rate of their next marketing offer.

YOU MUST ALSO KNOW

➢ Besides sophisticated methods of CHAID and logistic regression, one may also utilize the more popular RFM technique to identify the segments. RFM creates segments based on the recency, frequency and monetary value of purchase.

➢ While various sophisticated software options, such as SAS, SPSS, Minitab, etc., are available to perform predictive modelling, logistic regression can also be performed using R, which is available free of cost.

CHAPTER 8

THE MARKETING MIX

'Half the money I spend on advertising is wasted; the trouble is, I don't know which half.'

—John Wanamaker

This well-known saying by a famous US retailer, who lived a century ago, still reverberates strongly with the sentiments of present-day business managers and marketeers. Sukiran, who heads the marketing division of a leading apparel chain store in India, is facing a similar situation. As the competition in the industry is fierce, Sukiran has set up a marketing analytics division to guide him in the strategy to best advertise, promote and price his company's products. Over the past few years, he has spent millions of rupees in marketing activities such as advertisements, price discounts, etc., and through a variety of channels (television and radio advertisements). While the sales figures have shown an uptick during the investment period, a few questions continue to trouble Sukiran. He wonders how much the increased sales is due to his efforts and hence what is the actual return on the investments in marketing? Is there a better way to spend his budget—for example, spending more money in advertising through the radio than through TV? Would small but regular discounts have generated more sales than a one-time equivalent discount on price? Which of the factors among product, price and advertising is most effective in driving sales? What should be the optimal allocation of the marketing budget across these factors in the next marketing campaign?

Sukiran seeks the help of his newly set up marketing analytics team who collects data on past campaigns and promotions. He expects them to address his queries by using techniques such as marketing mix modelling.

MARKETING MIX MODELLING

Marketing mix refers to a mix of levers that marketeers use in order to influence the sales volume. The mix includes the four traditional Ps of marketing strategy, namely product, pricing, promotion (advertisements) and place (distribution). Marketeers can frequently change the levels of these levers, and hence the composition of the marketing mix, given the intensity of competition, macroeconomic conditions and growth targets. Since marketeers can change these levers when required, these levers are called controllable factors. There are additional factors, outside the influence of marketeers, which may also impact sales. These factors include seasonality, economy, competition, weather, and so on.

As there are a plethora of factors that influence sales, it becomes imperative for a marketeer to understand the effectiveness of each of the factors and then decide on the level of spending on the factors under control. This is where marketing mix modelling comes to the rescue. Marketing mix modelling applies the statistical techniques to answer a marketeer's questions as raised above by Sukiran, and hence provides a basis for data-driven decision-making. But before we dive into the models, it is important to understand some of the effects that are generated when a marketeer changes the level or mix of factors under control and how they may impact sales.

FIGURE 8.1: Marketing Funnel and Marketing Mix

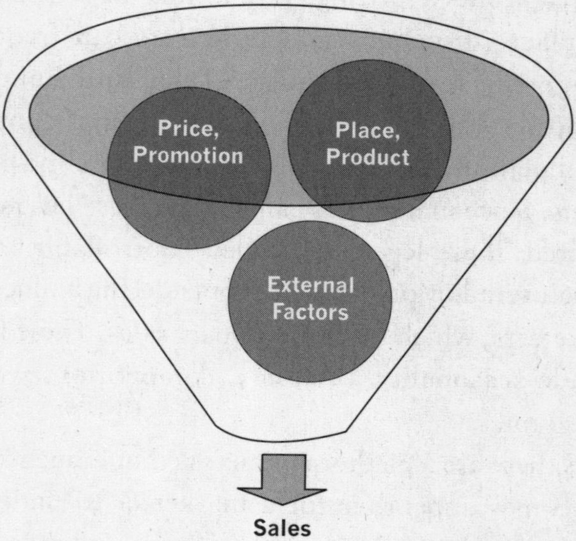

RESPONSE PATTERNS TO CHANGING MARKETING MIX

The market responds differently to the different levers of a marketing mix and generates sales patterns that are quite interesting to observe. For the ease of understanding these patterns, we will focus only on change in promotion (advertisements). This is also because the level of expenditure on advertising is in total control of the management and is discretionary in nature, whereas other levers of the marketing mix, such as product, may be compelled to change due to competitive forces or market demand.

Gerrard Tellis, in his paper 'Modeling Marketing Mix', identifies seven key patterns of response to advertisements. These are the current, shape, competitive, carryover, dynamic, content and media effects.[1]

The Current Effect

The current effect of advertising is the change in sales caused by the advertisement at the time when it is released in the market. In Figure 8.2, time is plotted on the X axis, sales on the Y axis, the time of advertisement by the up-arrows, baseline sales by the flat dotted line and the current effect by the sudden spikes in sales at the time of releasing the advertisement.

Empirical studies show that the current effect of advertisements is quite small relative to other marketing variables and hence care must be taken in modelling/analysing this effect so as not to exaggerate the 'fragile effect' of the advertisement.[2]

FIGURE 8.2: The Current Effect of Advertising

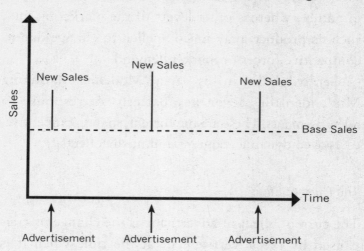

The Carryover Effect

The carryover effect of advertising is the change in current sales caused by past advertisements. This effect may occur due to a delayed response or delayed exposure to the advertisement, or an insufficient inventory to fulfil sales at the time of advertising. The carryover effect could be of a short or long duration, as depicted in Figures 8.3 and 8.4.

The total effect of advertising, then, can be estimated as the sum of current effect and carryover effect.

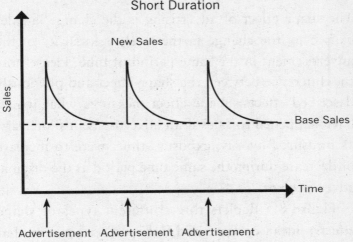

FIGURE 8.3: The Carryover Effect of Advertising—
Short Duration

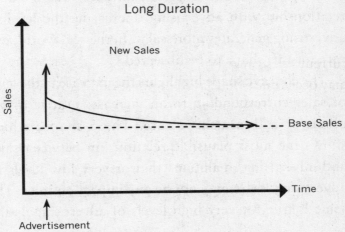

FIGURE 8.4: The Carryover Effect of Advertising—
Long Duration

The Shape Effect

The shape effect of advertising is the change in sales caused by the change in the level or intensity of the advertisement in the same period of time. Please note the difference between the shape effect and previously described effects. Shape effect measures what would have happened to sales if an advertisement's intensity, as measured by, say, exposure time, were to increase or decrease during the same time period as the original advertisement.

Figure 8.5 depicts three different types of shape effects: linear, concave and S-shaped. Please note that the X axis in this figure denotes the advertising level.

The linear shape depicts that sales has a linear relationship with advertising. Increasing the level of advertising generates more sales. In the real world, it is rare for this shape to be observed.

The concave shape highlights the increase in the level of sales corresponding to an increase in advertising, albeit at a diminishing rate. The S-shape, which shows the most plausible relationship between sales and advertising, maintains that at very low levels of advertising, there may not be any impact on sales. The same is true for very high levels of advertising as the gains in sales are minimal. Between the two extremes of advertising levels, sales first increase at an increasing rate and then increase at a diminishing rate, with an increase in the level of advertising.

FIGURE 8.5: The Shape Effect of Advertising

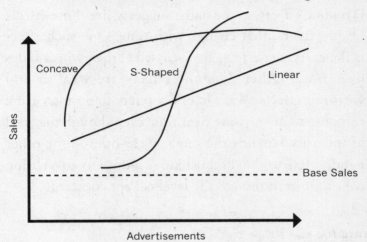

The Competitive Effect

The competitive effect of advertising arises due to the competition responding to a new innovation or advertisement by entering into the market with similar products or promotions. This dilutes the effectiveness of a company's advertisements. The company then needs to be careful to isolate the reaction and hence the impact due to competition before measuring the effectiveness of its advertising in generating sales.

Dynamic Effects

Dynamic effects, as the name suggests, are those effects of advertising that change with time. One such effect is the carryover effect, as discussed earlier, which fades over time. Other dynamic effects are wear-in and wear-out effects. Wear-in effect refers to an increasing response to advertising over time even though the level of intensity remains the same. Wear-out, on the other hand, refers to the diminishing response to advertising over time even though the level is kept constant.

The Content Effect

The content effect refers to the change in sales caused by a change in the content of the advertisement. Since this is an important source of variation in advertisement responsiveness, marketeers keep trying with this aspect of advertising and bring innovation into the way they connect with consumers.

The Media Effect

The media effect refers to the variation in advertisement responsiveness due to the type of media used for advertising such as TV, radio, magazine, newspaper, billboards, etc. Not all media types are equally effective in generating a sales response and hence marketeers try with a mix of media types to optimize sales response behaviour, given their target consumer set.

*

Now, let's turn our attention back to marketing mix modelling and how it can be used to answer the questions raised by Sukiran.

Marketing mix modelling is a term used for a broad range of statistical models that use historical data to determine the strength and degree of the relationship between sales and various marketing mix activities such as advertising, promotion, price, and so on. Once the relationship is established, it is utilized to forecast the future level of sales, given the spending on marketing mix variables, and also to determine the optimal allocation of spending across various mix variables.

There are various statistical techniques used for

marketing mix modelling; however, the most popular among them is the multiple linear regression.[3] This technique is based on a number of independent variables (in our case, marketing mix variables, besides others) and how they relate to the dependent variable (sales in our case). Once the model is built with a certain level of accuracy and is validated on an independent sample of data, the results of the model can be used to analyse the contribution of each of the independent variables (marketing activity) on sales pattern. The analysis highlights the incremental gains in sales of per-unit spending on each of the marketing activities. Sukiran can also calculate the return on marketing investment for each of the marketing activities carried out during the period. Then, the marketing manager can use this information to optimally allocate his marketing budget across activities.

In the simplest form, the regression equation can be expressed as

Sales = α + β Var 1 + γ Var 2 + . . . + Error

where

α reflects the level of sales when all other variables in the equation are at zero level

β reflects the impact on sales for a unit change in variable Var 1

γ reflects the impact on sales for a unit change in variable Var 2

and so on.

The success of marketing mix modelling depends heavily on the availability of internal and external data for analysis as well as the appropriate level and quality of the data. Companies must invest in building infrastructure to capture historical information so that it's readily available for future use.

As mentioned before, multiple variables, controllable or uncontrollable, can form part of the regression equation as long as they significantly impact the sales pattern of a firm or business. Hence, one must be careful in selecting the possible factors given the industry context, competition and product type or market characteristics. For example, apparel sales, especially woollen, have a strong seasonal pattern and hence may depend upon the weather conditions and the geography. Taking another example, in an industry where aftersales service plays a critical role—such as the speed of installation of an air conditioner—an indicator to capture service levels driving sales can become part of the regression equation.

Using the technique to solve Sukiran's problem, let's start by looking at the dependent variable—apparel sales in our case. Sukiran's team has access to the sales data of the last three years (2009–11) on a monthly basis. The data is aggregated at a national level; however, one can perform the analysis at a regional level for better predictions and effective use of differentiated marketing activities across regions.

Sukiran had spent around Rs 200 million (or 20 crore) in six TV campaigns in the past three years, with each campaign lasting around three to six weeks. The campaigns were aired at the beginning of every six-month window, starting in January 2009.

In addition, around Rs 175 million (or 17.5 crore) were spent on radio advertisements spread over the entire three years.

The marketing team had also conducted a couple of sales promotion events, one in December 2009 giving a discount of 15 per cent on sales value and another in February 2011 with the offer of 'Buy 5, get 3 free' as part of their Mega Promo activity.

Also, the price of the apparel was raised gradually over the three-year period to cover the increased cost of raw material and labour (see Figure 8.6 for a graphic illustration of these activities).

FIGURE 8.6: Case Study of Sales, Price and Marketing Activity

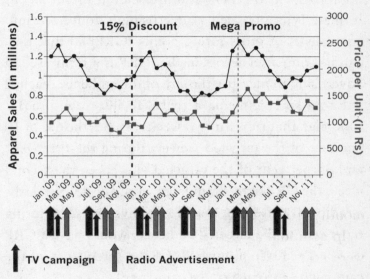

The questions that now remain are how much of the sales behaviour is explained by each of the marketing activities and what is the return on investment due to these activities?

Before we subject our raw data to regression modelling to answer these questions, we need to ensure that the data is in the right format for use. Our dependent-variable sales is measured in million units sold per month and is suitable for use. However, variables such as TV campaigns and radio advertisements are in rupees millions spent on them and are seldom useful in this format. Typically, media advertising is converted into equivalents of gross rating points (GRP) so that they can be compared across media. GRP is a term used in advertising to measure the size of the audience reached due to a specific media activity. To illustrate, if a TV campaign that runs for two weeks catches the eye of 10 per cent of the targeted viewers during the first week and 35 per cent of the targeted viewers in the second week, the GRP of this campaign would be 45. Similarly, a radio advertisement that is aired five times, capturing 6 per cent of the targeted audience, would have a GRP of $5 \times 6 = 30$. In a nutshell, GRP = (Frequency of the campaign) $\times$ (Reach of the campaign).

Also, variables such as promotions are represented by an indicator variable taking a value of 1 when the promotion takes place and 0 otherwise. Such indicator variables would represent the '15 per cent discount' and 'Mega Promo' events in our case study.

Gross Rating Points (GRP) = Reach × Frequency of a campaign expressed as percentages.

GRP values can be greater than 100 per cent since duplicate counts of the targeted population, generated through multiple runs of the same campaign, form part of the 'Gross' calculation.

Looking at the sales behaviour, one may find patterns such as an uptick in sales during the month of February and a downward movement during August. There could also be an impact of seasonality on sales behaviour, which would be captured by indicator variables representing the different seasons in the regression equation.

Since the sales of apparel are maximum during the festival months of September, October and November, an indicator variable (seasonality) is used, which takes the value of 1 for these three months and 0 for the other months. Now, running a multiple regression on the data yields the following relationship between sales and other variables

Sales = 120,250 + 145 × TV + 450 × Promotion + 4580 × Seasonality + 181 × Radio − 80 × Price

Note that the coefficients of all the variables are positive except for price, signifying that TV, radio and promotion had a positive impact on sales while price had a negative impact, as one would expect.

With these coefficients, it is easy to derive the sales impact due to a particular variable when the other variables are held constant. For example, the total TV GRP for three years was 2896; multiplying this with the coefficient for TV, 145, yields 419,920. This can be seen as the number of apparel units that would be sold due to the TV campaign if the other variables remain constant. One can also convert these units into a revenue figure by multiplying by an average price, Rs 1154 in our example. This generates a total revenue of Rs 484 million. Taking it a step further, to calculate the return on investment on the TV campaign, divide the revenue by the Rs 200 million that were spent on TV campaigns. This gives a value of 2.42 implying that 2.42 rupees were gained for every rupee spent on TV campaigns.

Sukiran's team did this number crunching for the radio campaign as well and found that radio advertisements generated a total revenue of Rs 350 million with a total return on investment of 2: Rs 350 million (revenue)/ Rs 175 million (investment).

Since the return on investment on TV advertisements

is higher than the return on radio ads, Sukiran's team can increase the investment in TV advertisements till the time the incremental (marginal) return on TV remains higher than radio. This reallocation of the marketing budget will increase the overall return on investment.

Now, to answer the question as to how much of the sales behaviour is dependent on price, one can calculate the price elasticity of demand using the coefficient of price from the regression equation using the formula

Elasticity = (Average Price/Average Sales) × Coefficient

for our case,

Elasticity = (1150/1.02 million) × −80 = −0.09

This implies that an 11 per cent decrease in price will increase sales by 1 per cent.

Thus, with marketing mix modelling, Sukiran has been able to analyse the effectiveness of his marketing activities and how sales behaviour is triggered by price changes. He has now become more adept at optimally allocating his marketing budget across the different activities (advertisements, promotions, etc.), given his sales target for the next quarter.

SUMMARY

Marketing mix modelling is a powerful tool which, if used effectively, can help determine the strength and the degree of relationship between sales and various marketing activities such as promotion, advertising, pricing, and so on. Once the strength of the relationship is determined, a business can gain significant returns on their marketing investment by choosing the appropriate kind and level of marketing activities. Needless to say, the type and quality of historical business data plays a critical role in determining the accuracy and strength of such relationships.

REFERENCES

1. Shaun Doyle, 'Which Part of My Marketing Spend Really Works? Marketing Mix Modelling may have an answer', available online at http://www.il-synergy.com/html_he/articles/Marketing_Mix_Modelling.pdf.
2. Gerard J. Tellis, 'Modeling Marketing Mix', in Rajiv Grover and Marco Vriens, *The Handbook of Marketing Research: Uses, Misuses, and Future Advances* (California: Sage Publications, 2006), pp 506–22.
3. 'Advertising adstock', Wikipedia.org, http://en.wikipedia.org/wiki/Advertising_adstock (accessed 17 March 2012).

CHAPTER 9

TOO MUCH OR TOO LITTLE?

Shikha is an entrepreneur and runs a medium-size pastry shop in downtown Bengaluru. She has successfully built her business by providing excellent customer service and quality of products. Today, her shop displays more than fifty varieties of pastries and cakes. Shikha boasts of running a business that attracts not only the average shopper on the street but also the large corporate houses that place orders for her sumptuous treats.

While Shikha is content with the business performance and the popularity it has gained over the past five years, she wonders if she can manage business operations in a better way, especially during the Christmas season when she faces the toughest challenge of her forecasting abilities—How many cakes of each variety should be produced? If she were to produce less than the demand during Christmas time, she would lose out on potential business. If she produces more than required, there will be an unwanted inventory of cakes, which she will then have to dispose of or sell at a discount. Either way, she would incur a loss, and so there is a need to find a balance.

Till date, Shikha has been using heuristics in determining the quantity produced based on the average demand for each type of cake as observed over the years. However, every year she has seen either an overproduction or underproduction. She is fully aware of the fact that she will never be able to exactly match supply with demand, and she is concerned whether using such heuristics is maximizing her profits or not. Somewhere, she feels that there must be a better way of deciding the optimal levels of production. Right now, her decisions are yielding either too much or too little.

THE NEWSVENDOR MODEL PROBLEM

One can associate two key features with the challenge that Shikha faces above. Firstly, she has to decide on the production quantity in the wake of uncertain demand. To make matters interesting, she cannot even adjust the quantity produced quickly enough to meet the demand if customers are at the shop when she does not have enough cakes on the shelf. So underproduction means lost opportunity and hence lower profits. Secondly, the product under question is perishable, that is, it has a short shelf life. If there is an overproduction of cakes, she cannot store the unsold cakes for more than a day with a view to selling them on other days.

In simple terms, there is a potential benefit and potential loss associated with producing a certain quantity of cakes (the word 'potential' signifies the uncertainty involved in the demand). The objective is to find the optimal quantity of cakes at which profits can be maximized.

To help her out of the problem, Shikha takes assistance from a friend who works in an analytics industry, specializing in operations management. Her friend tells Shikha about the newsvendor model that can solve challenges with features similar to the ones faced by her.

The newsvendor model derives its name from a typical problem that all newsvendors face every morning, that is, to determine the optimal quantity of newspapers they should keep at the shop. If the quantity of newspapers stored is less than the demand during the day, it would result in a loss of potential sale. On the flip side, if the quantity stored is more than that day's demand, newsvendors would suffer a loss as that day's newspaper would be just a piece of paper tomorrow and would have no value. Here, again, newsvendors have to determine the optimal quantity of newspapers that will maximize their profits for the day.[1]

The next section takes a closer look at the model and applies it to Shikha's challenge.

FIGURE 9.1: A Manifestation of the Newsvendor Problem

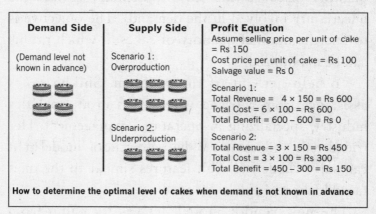

Demand Side	Supply Side	Profit Equation
		Assume selling price per unit of cake = Rs 150
(Demand level not known in advance)	Scenario 1: Overproduction	Cost price per unit of cake = Rs 100 Salvage value = Rs 0
		Scenario 1: Total Revenue = 4 × 150 = Rs 600 Total Cost = 6 × 100 = Rs 600 Total Benefit = 600 – 600 = Rs 0
	Scenario 2: Underproduction	Scenario 2: Total Revenue = 3 × 150 = Rs 450 Total Cost = 3 × 100 = Rs 300 Total Benefit = 450 – 300 = Rs 150

How to determine the optimal level of cakes when demand is not known in advance

The Marginal Rule

In order to determine the optimal quantity of production that maximizes the expected profit, four key inputs are required—demand forecast and its distribution, cost price per unit of product, sale price per unit and the salvage value per unit.

For demand forecast and its distribution, Shikha uses the actual quantity demanded in the previous three years during the Christmas season as shown in Column A of Table 9.1. The second column highlights the probability of a particular level of demand, calculated based on the frequency at which that level of demand was observed compared to other levels.

The third column reflects the cumulative probability by simply cumulating the second column for the various levels of demand. This is used to determine the probability of demand less than or equal to a certain level. For example, from Table 9.1 it can be observed that the probability of cake demand less than or equal to 3 is 0.35 (0.15 + 0.10 + 0.10) and the probability of cake demand less than or equal to 5 is 0.70 (0.15 + 0.10 + 0.10 + 0.10 + 0.15 + 0.20).

For notational purposes, we depict this probability distribution function as $F(Q)$, where $F(Q)$ is the probability of demand being lower than or equal to Q.

So, $F(2) = 0.25$, $F(3) = 0.35$, and so on.

The fourth column, then, complements the third column. It reflects the probability of demand being greater than a particular level and is calculated by subtracting F(Q) from 1 (since the probability of demand less than or equal to a given quantity plus the probability of demand greater than the same given quantity must equal 1).

So, the probability of demand greater than 3 = 1 − F(3) = 1 − 0.35 = 0.65.

TABLE 9.1: The Historical Distribution of Cake Demand

Level of cake demand (in units of 100) (A)	Probability (B)	F(Q) = Probability of demand <=Q units (C)	1 − F(Q) = Probability of demand >Q units (D)
1	0.15	0.15	0.85
2	0.10	0.25	0.75
3	0.10	0.35	0.65
4	0.15	0.50	0.50
5	0.20	0.70	0.30
6	0.30	1.00	0.00

Since Shikha has not added any new variety of cake this year nor changed the quality/pricing of any product, she believes that the historical distribution of cake demand is going to hold good for the upcoming Christmas season and hence is ready to use this empirical data for estimating this year's demand.

Demand forecasting is a critical input in determining the optimal level of production, and care must be taken while generating the demand distribution function.

In scenarios of change in product line, aggressive marketing strategy compared to previous years, improved purchasing power of consumers or any other factor having a considerable bearing on the demand compared to previous years, actual historical demand may not present a true picture of this year's demand.

Demand distribution described in this case is a 'discrete' demand distribution where the probability for a discrete level of demand can be read from the table, but only for the levels captured by it. In some cases, it may be convenient to assume a continuous distribution like normal or log-normal distribution as the demand distribution.

So much for the demand distribution. Now let's focus on the other three inputs required to determine the optimal quantity of cake production.

The first one is sale price per unit. This is the money earned per unit of product by selling it in the market. For the cake problem, let's assume the sale price per unit of cake is Rs 200.

The second input required is cost price per unit. This is the money spent on producing a single unit. In case the product is procured from the supplier and not produced internally, the cost price will also include any packaging or insurance cost paid while procuring that unit of product. For the cake problem, let's assume the cost price per unit of cake to be Rs 100.

Lastly, we require the salvage value of a product. This is the money recovered by selling the product at a discount in case the product is not in demand—either because it is outdated or simply because it was overproduced. For the cake problem, let's assume the salvage value as 0 since spoilt cakes don't earn anything.

Let's assume that Shikha has produced Q units of cake and she is 100 per cent sure that these will be sold. In this scenario, we can calculate her total benefit by selling these Q units as

The salvage value of a product, defined as the value that can be recovered from the units that couldn't be sold, can be positive, zero or negative.

At times, one may have to pay to get the leftover units disposed of, resulting in a negative salvage value.

Total Benefit from selling Q units = Q × (Selling Price per unit – Cost Price per unit)

Now, Shikha is contemplating producing 1 additional unit of the product. She is not sure whether it would be sold.

In the scenario when an additional unit gets sold, the marginal benefit (benefit due to producing that additional unit) can be calculated as Selling Price – Cost Price. The marginal benefit can also be seen as an opportunity lost when the demand for the additional unit existed but the producer did not make it available. This opportunity lost due to under-stocking is referred to as the Underage Cost (denoted by C_u).

Assuming that the selling price per unit of cake is

Rs 150 and the cost price per unit Rs 100, the marginal benefit or underage cost will be Rs 150 – Rs 100 = Rs 50.

In a scenario where the additional unit remains unsold, the marginal loss (loss due to producing that additional unit) can be calculated as Cost Price – Salvage Value. Please note that the marginal loss will be lower than the cost price in case she is able to recover some money by selling that unit at a lower price (salvage value). The marginal loss is also referred to as the Overage Cost (denoted by C_o) because it signifies the cost due to overstocking that additional unit when the demand did not exist.

Assuming the salvage value of cake to be 0 and the cost price to be Rs 100, the marginal loss or overage cost will be Rs 100 – 0 = Rs 100.

For Shikha to decide whether she should stock this additional unit, she needs to evaluate the *expected* marginal benefit with the *expected* marginal cost. The expected marginal benefit is calculated by multiplying marginal benefit with the probability that the additional unit will be sold; and the expected marginal cost is calculated by multiplying the marginal cost with the probability that the additional unit will not be sold.

Only if the expected marginal benefit from producing

an additional unit is greater than the expected marginal loss should Shikha produce that additional unit. She should continue producing additional units until the expected marginal benefit equals the expected marginal cost from an additional unit. That is to say, the optimal quantity would be one where both the expected benefit and expected loss are equal at the margin.

This is referred to as the 'marginal rule of optimal production in case of uncertain demand'.

But What Is the Intuition behind This Rule?

As one keeps on producing the additional unit, the probability of selling it keeps decreasing. Hence the expected marginal benefit keeps falling with an increase in production. Conversely, as one adds an additional unit to production, the probability of that unit remaining unsold keeps increasing. Hence the expected marginal loss keeps increasing with increase in production. The optimal level of quantity that maximizes profits (or net benefits) would then be one where the expected marginal benefit and expected marginal loss are the same. Beyond that production level, the expected marginal loss would be more than the expected marginal benefit, thus lowering the overall benefit of production.

This is shown in Table 9.2, which builds on Table 9.1 by adding columns E and F. The expected marginal loss (Column E) keeps increasing because the probability of demand less than or equal to the unit produced keeps increasing with an increase in production (F(Q) in Column C). On the other hand, the expected marginal benefit (Column F) keeps falling because the probability of demand greater than the units produced keeps falling with an increase in production (1 − F(Q) in Column D).

From Table 9.2, what should Shikha choose as the optimal level of production? At a production level of 1, the expected marginal benefit (42.5) is greater than the expected marginal loss (15), hence level 1 should be produced. What about level 2? Here again, the expected marginal benefit is greater than the expected marginal loss (37.5 > 25). However, from level 4 onward the expected losses are greater than the expected benefit. Hence level 3 is the optimum level of production that maximizes profits.

The same result can be derived mathematically. To maximize profits, the marginal rule states that

Expected Marginal Benefit = Expected Marginal Loss

Now, the expected marginal benefit for Qth quantity of production can be calculated as (Equation 1):

$$(1 - F(Q)) \times (\text{Selling Price} - \text{Cost Price}) = (1 - F(Q)) \times C_u$$

In simple words, the expected marginal benefit of producing a unit is the probability of that unit getting sold (which will occur when the demand is greater than Q) multiplied by the net benefit derived by selling it (its underage cost).

Similarly, the expected marginal loss for Qth quantity of production can be calculated as (Equation 2):

$$F(Q) \times (\text{Cost Price} - \text{Salvage Value}) = F(Q) \times C_o$$

In other words, the expected marginal loss of producing a unit is the probability of that unit not getting sold multiplied by the net loss derived by producing it (its overage cost).

Equating equations 1 and 2 above,

$(1 - F(Q)) \times C_u = F(Q) \times C_o$ and rearranging this yields $F(Q^*) = C_u / (C_u + C_o)$ where Q^* is the optimal level of production

TABLE 9.2: Calculating Expected Marginal Benefit and Loss
for a Given Level of Production

Level of cake demand (in units of 100) (A)	Probabi- lity (B)	F(Q) = Probabi- lity of demand <=Q units (C)	1–F(Q) = Probabi- lity of demand >Q units (D)	Expected marginal loss of producing Qth unit (E=C×100) in Rs	Expected marginal benefit of producing Qth unit (F=D×50) in Rs
1	0.15	0.15	0.85	15	42.5
2	0.10	0.25	0.75	25	37.5
3	0.10	0.35	0.65	35	32.5
4	0.15	0.50	0.50	50	25
5	0.20	0.70	0.30	70	15
6	0.30	1.00	0.00	100	0

FIGURE 9.2: The Marginal Rule of Optimal Production Level
in Case of Uncertain Demand

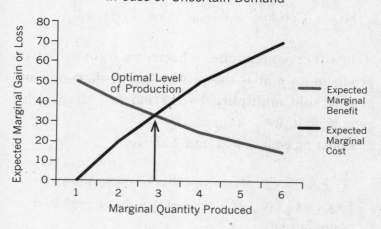

The ratio on the right side of the above equation is also known as the 'critical ratio'. One can find the optimal level of production by calculating the critical ratio and then finding out the level of demand (Q^*) for which $F(Q^*)$ equals the critical ratio.

For Shikha,

$C_u = 150 - 100 = 50$ and $C_o = 100 - 0 = 100$, hence
Critical Ratio $= 50/(50 + 100) = 0.33$.

Referring to Table 9.2, the level of demand at which $F(Q)$ is close to 0.33 is level 3 (at $Q = 3$, $F(Q) = 0.35$). This is the same result that we had arrived at earlier by comparing marginal benefits and losses manually for each level of demand.

Figure 9.2 presents a graphical view of the marginal rule for the optimal level of production.

YOU MUST ALSO KNOW

➤ There are numerous applications of the newsvendor model in a variety of fields, such as revenue management in airlines or in the hotel industry.

➤ An example of the application of this model would be deciding the optimal level(s) of discounted fare with a view to the fixed supply of seats on a particular flight.

➤ In the airlines industry, 'yield management' refers to the use of such models in maximizing revenue. American Airlines in the late 1980s used these techniques to derive an estimated benefit of more than $1.4 billion over a three-year period.[2]

CHAPTER 10

IS THE PROCESS UNDER CONTROL?

Narayan owns a business that produces USB drives for a multinational computer manufacturer. His factory hosts state-of-the-art technology and employs the best brains from premier engineering institutes in India. On average, his factory produces 1000 USB drives every day, which are accumulated and sent out to the manufacturer at the end of every month.

Before sending out the consignment, a quality check is done to ensure that critical features of the USB drive, such as its width, will be acceptable to the manufacturer. While the process of producing the drives is quite standard and automated, Narayan, at times, finds some variation in the dimensions of the USB drives. This variation could be due to various reasons such as quality of raw materials used, prevailing factory conditions (temperature, voltage, etc.) or just sheer chance that the machine produced an output slightly different from the previous one.

Till date Narayan has neither seen a single consignment getting rejected at the manufacturer's end, nor has he discarded the output himself; however, he is worried that the excessive variation in the dimensions of the USB drives may cause loss of revenue in the future.

Narayan wonders if he can build an early warning system to gauge whether the USB drive production process is in control or out of control. Instead of checking the output just before the consignment is delivered, is there a system that can alert him as to whether the production is going smoothly or he needs to intervene? What could be the basis of such a system? Should the system review the production on an hourly basis, a daily basis or at some other frequency? How much variation should the system tag as 'in control' and how much should be classified as 'out of control'? What remedial actions should be taken once a process is identified as out of control? These are some of the questions that Narayan is seeking the answers to.

VARIATION, CAUSES AND STATISTICAL PROCESS CONTROL CHARTS

Almost a century ago, Dr Walter Shewhart, employed in Bell Telephone Laboratories, was troubled by questions akin to those Narayan is facing today. In the 1920s, Dr Shewhart researched the ways to manage and improve quality and developed statistical process control (SPC) charts that would guide him regarding whether a process is in control or not. Dr W. Edwards Deming built upon Dr Shewhart's work and took the SPC charts to Japan post–Second World War, where he revolutionized the way quality was perceived.

Before delving into the SPC charts, let's understand variation and its possible causes. It is a simple truth that variation is universal, whether in products developed by machines or things created by nature. Would you ever find two identical mangoes on the same tree? Similarly, an artist may not be able to replicate the exact expressions on a painting as he depicted on his previous one. Or, a favourite cake recipe yields a slightly different taste each time it is used. Thus, variation is omnipresent and an inherent part of everyday life.

Now let's look at what could have caused these variations. In the artist's example above, one simple reason for the painting to have turned out slightly different is the fact that it was painted on a different day; it was natural that the result too would be slightly different. Nobody expects exactly the same output from an artist each time. Such reasons for variations are referred to as due to 'natural or common' causes.

Now consider a scenario where the painting turned out to be substantially different in comparison with a previous work because the painter used a coarse canvas as against a finer one that he used every day. This highlights a fundamental change to the process— something very special that has caused the variation. Such reasons for variation are referred to as 'special or assignable' causes, because one can assign an objective reason for the difference.

How does one decide whether a variation is natural or special? This is where SPC charts provide assistance.

A statistical process control chart gives a visual representation of the output characteristic measured over time (USB width in Narayan's case) and, *on a statistical basis*, draws upper and lower control limits for the same. Any point outside the control limits is then identified as variation due to a special cause and the process is tagged as out of control and corrective action is required. Any point within the limits is considered variation due to a normal cause and, in general, one need not worry about it. A typical SPC chart would have time on the X axis, output characteristic measured on the Y axis, three lines (one central and two control lines) and a trend line of the measured characteristic as represented in Figure 10.1.

FIGURE 10.1: Sample Statistical Process Control Chart

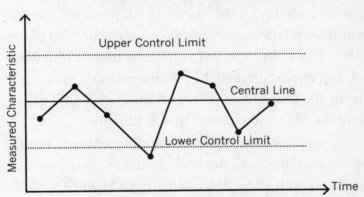

THE METHOD TO DRAW A STATISTICAL PROCESS CONTROL (SPC) CHART

Let's review the method to draw an SPC chart by focusing on Narayan's challenge at hand. Narayan is worried about the variation in the width of the USB drives produced at his factory. In order to gauge the extent of the variation, he starts recording the width of the drives produced each day. Since it will be time-consuming to review all 1000 drives produced daily, Narayan takes a random sample of 50 drives and records the width for fifteen days, as shown in Table 10.1.[1]

The average width for a day is calculated in the last column by taking a simple average of the width of 50 drives for that day. These are plotted on the Y axis against each day on the X axis. In addition, the average width for all the days is calculated at the bottom of the table. This is the expected average width of a USB drive on any day (represented by μ, pronounced *mew*) and forms the central line on the chart. For all USB drives over the fifteen-day period, $\mu = 8.42$ mm.

Now comes the task of creating control limits. Without getting into the background statistics, control limits are formed by first calculating a factor $3 \times \sigma/\sqrt{N}$, where σ represents a standard deviation of USB drive width across the days and N is the size of the daily sample, which is 50 in our case.

Now, the upper control limit (UCL) is calculated by adding this factor to μ, while the lower control limit (LCL) is found by subtracting this factor from μ. In our example, UCL = 8.71 mm and LCL = 8.13 mm (see Figure 10.2).

TABLE 10.1: USB Drive Width Data for Calculation
of Average

Day	Width of USB1	Width of USB2	Width of USB3	...	Width of USB50	Average Width for a Day
1	8.55	8.74	8.57		8.62	8.45
2	8.74	8.90	8.76		8.80	8.60
3	8.47	8.59	8.49		8.52	8.30
4	8.70	8.79	8.72		8.74	8.50
5	9.14	9.22	9.16		9.18	8.92
6	8.48	8.53	8.50		8.51	8.24
7	8.71	8.75	8.73		8.73	8.45
8	8.60	8.61	8.62		8.61	8.32
9	8.42	8.42	8.44		8.42	8.12
10	8.87	8.85	8.89		8.87	8.55
11	8.90	8.87	8.92		8.90	8.57
12	8.76	8.71	8.78		8.75	8.41
13	8.75	8.69	8.77		8.74	8.39
14	8.49	8.41	8.51		8.47	8.12
15	8.71	8.62	8.73		8.68	8.32
						$\mu = 8.42$

The control limits are also referred to as the 3-sigma limits (note the multiplication by the number 3 in the factor calculated above). These control limits or boundaries are expected to hold 99.73 per cent of all the daily averages when the process variation is part of the normal process design. This comes from the property of the normal distribution that a 3-sigma interval around the mean will capture around 99.73 per cent of the observations.[2]

Conversely, there is only a 0.23 per cent chance that any value would fall outside the limits in the normal course of process operation. And hence, daily average values falling outside the control limits require further investigation and signal the occurrence of the special cause variation.

In Figure 10.2, for Narayan, the value for Day 5 falls outside the UCL and hence the process is tagged as out of control and requires further investigation.

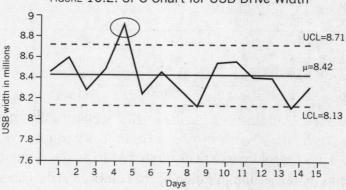

FIGURE 10.2: SPC Chart for USB Drive Width

THE NEXT STEPS

Now suppose that Narayan has identified a condition where the USB drive production process has gone out of control. He needs to delve into the process and understand the root cause of the variation. All sub-steps in the process need to be critically reviewed to check if a fundamental change has crept in without being noticed. For example, it may be that suppliers are providing varying quality of raw materials over a period, or the temperature under which a raw material is processed has been kept too high (or low) compared to the specified level, and so on.

At the end of the in-depth analysis, one of two inferences may emerge. One could be that the process (or sub-steps) has been changed fundamentally. This inference would require changing the process (sub-step) and a re-evaluation of the process to keep the output within control.

The second inference could be that the process (or sub-steps) is being followed as per design and there is no fundamental change to it. In this scenario, all one can say is that Narayan was plain unlucky to observe one value outside the control limits as there was only a 0.23 per cent chance that it would occur in the normal situation. However, he should be satisfied that he has carried out a thorough investigation to ensure that his process is in control.

The SPC chart produced above using the mean (average value) is commonly referred to as the X-bar chart, because in statistics the mean of a variable is, generally, represented as a bar on that variable.

- An SPC chart can leverage variable data in continuous form (as illustrated through the USB width example) or attribute data in discrete form (such as faulty or fair medical diagnosis). However, the type of SPC charts (C chart, NP chart, etc.) used for attribute data would be different from those used for continuous data (mean chart, range chart, etc.).

- Early warning limits can also be set at 2-sigma limits as against the default 3-sigma limits. However, the chances of calling a process out of control, when in fact it is not, increase when the limits are put at a lower sigma level.

- Violation rules: in addition to the rule that flags a process as out of control when a value is outside the 3-sigma control limits other statistical rules exist, defined in the *AT&T Statistical Quality*

Control Handbook, that guide the decision to call a process under control or not. There is a rule which says that if there is a series of six points that are successively higher or lower, then the process is potentially out of control or, in other words, there are special causes of variation.

The control chart analysis depends critically on the quality of information provided for the analysis. For example, if input data on USB width is not measured accurately and consistently, control charts may highlight the process to be out of control. Due respect must be given to the information measurement system so that one is not trapped in a 'garbage in, garbage out' analysis.

Control limits have no relationship with the specification limits as desired by the customer, and hence an SPC chart analysis will not show whether the process is meeting the customer's requirements or not. A different analysis, known as

!

process capability analysis, is required to adjudge the process output against the specifications.

Control limits are statistically driven, based on the observed data, while specification limits by the customer are dictated outside the process.

YOU MUST ALSO KNOW

➤ Besides SPC charts, other quality management techniques, such as continuous improvements, 6-sigma methodology, design of experiments, and so on, are quite popular and have yielded tremendous results for the manufacturing and services industries alike.

➤ Tata Steel India became the first integrated steel company outside Japan to be awarded the Deming Application Prize in 2008 for adoption of Total Quality Management practices and delivering on excellent quality.

➤ General Electric (GE), is known worldwide for delivering unmatched quality of products and services. GE imbibed the 6 sigma into its culture after the technique was originally developed by Motorola in 1986.

CHAPTER 11

INVESTING IN TALENT

Things have not been going well at Ringer's for the last two years. Every now and then, the brightest middle managers exit the company. In the last meeting of the board, the CFO in his report highlighted this and showed how talent-acquisition costs have grown by more than 50 per cent in the last two years. The HR director explained that the high turnover of middle management executives within two years of joining was pushing up talent-acquisition costs and hindering operational efficiency. The board then spends a considerable amount of time trying to understand the reason for such behaviour and mandates Roma to find a way out of this problem.

Roma, who has been with Ringer's for over a decade

and is leading the HR operations, analyses the exit interviews to find the potential causes. The interviews uniformly highlight the 'lack of career development opportunities' as the main reason for quitting the company. Roma finds in this a chance to execute one of her long-cherished plans—a leadership programme for middle managers. She had suggested this to the company leadership a couple of times before, but did not find support as it was found to be very costly. However, now with talent-acquisition costs gradually rising she feels that the time is ripe to implement her plan. She intends to tie up with the best management institute in the country to deliver this leadership programme. Her plan is to induct high-potential middle managers into the programme after they complete one year in the organization. The programme would be spread over two years and would be divided into a number of modules. Each module of the programme would equip them with some of the cutting-edge management concepts. In addition, it would form a group of high performers who can communicate with one another and solve problems which require interdepartmental coordination. It is clear to Roma that the benefits to be derived from this programme would far outweigh the costs.

COST–BENEFIT ANALYSIS

A week later Roma meets the CEO, Jim, with her plan for the middle management leadership programme. After a detailed presentation on the costs and benefits of the programme, Roma seeks Jim's approval to proceed further. A few moments of silence greet Roma as Jim seems to be lost in thought. Collecting his thoughts Jim says that while the presentation was good he has some concerns. He is worried about how the managers for this leadership programme would be selected. About 40 per cent of the company's employees have been with the company for more than a decade. If the programme is primarily aimed at new employees with only one year experience, it is quite likely that the loyal employees who have been with the company for a long time would feel dissatisfied and excluded. The negative feelings of this group may adversely impact the success of the leadership programme. Additionally, the kind of leadership programme required for the loyal group would be quite different and it would be inappropriate to put them through the same training. He is also concerned about the cost–benefit analysis being projected by Roma. To Jim, the cost figures appear quite large and concrete whereas the benefits figures are tentative. Jim wants

Roma to work more on the proposal and come back to him with a well-defined method of evaluating the return on investment (ROI) of the leadership training programme.

As Roma grapples with the problem of evaluating the ROI on training, she happens to meet her old friend Brij. They had been together in their MBA programme and had not been in touch for some time. Recently Brij accepted an offer from a US-based company for the role of chief learning officer (CLO) of its India operations. Brij contacted Roma over a social networking site and they decided to meet for coffee. After recalling many cherished memories of their university days, beloved and detestable professors, the crushes and the heartaches, Roma asks Brij whether he has ever attempted to evaluate the ROI on training. Brij smiles and says, 'Attempted, yes, several times. But I doubt whether I ever got it right.' Roma is encouraged—even if an imprecise ROI can be calculated, it may save her pet leadership training programme project. She decides to invite Brij for a discussion at her office the next week.

Brij explains to Roma and her team Kirkpatrick's four-level training evaluation model.[1] The levels in this model are reaction, learning, behaviour and results. The first level, 'reaction', measures how well the trainees reacted to the training. This information is captured in the 'happy sheets' that are filled out by the trainees immediately after the training. Such sheets ask how the trainees felt about the instructor, the topic of training, material, pedagogy, venue, etc. The second level, 'learning', measures how much the trainees have learnt. To evaluate the extent of learning due to the training, a 'pre-test' is taken on the topics related to the training and then a 'post-test' is taken at the end of the training. The difference in the pre- and post-test scores gives an idea of how much learning happened due to the training. The third level, 'behaviour', measures the extent to which the trainees' behaviour has changed based on the training received. Specifically, this looks at how the trainees apply the information gained during the training in their job situation. The final level, 'results', measures the impact of the training on the attainment of the overall goals of the organization and on its bottom line.

Roma asks Brij how to measure results, since that is the most important thing for the computation of ROI. Brij replies that while the measurements of reaction and learning can be made quite accurately, following appropriate procedures, the measurement of behaviour has to be done using actual observational data. For that, appropriate metrics need to be set up prior to the training

FIGURE 11.1: Kirkpatrick's Four-Level Training Model

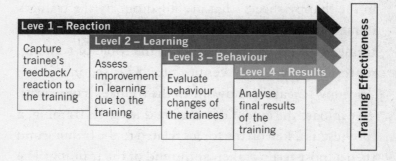

and the baseline measurements for these metrics need to be taken. Some time after the training (say three or six months), the same metrics need to be measured again, and the difference in the value of the metrics can serve as an indicator of the extent of behaviour change. Measuring behaviour change can be quite complex, and careful planning is required to get a good idea about the same. 'Unfortunately, the most difficult measurement is that of the results,' says Brij. 'The results related to a specific training are very difficult to isolate from other business factors like changes in business environment, business decisions encouraging or discouraging certain activities, availability of jobs that use the contents discussed in the training, other related trainings, etcetera.' Moreover, for some career trainings, like the leadership training that

Roma is thinking about, the benefits to the organization may accrue over a long period of time and it may require a huge effort to capture all the benefits. Thus, often the ROI for training is not well estimated.

Roma thinks over the problem for a few days and discusses it with her team. After a lot of discussions, the team decide to take a three-year horizon for observing a change in the behavioural metrics. They decide to focus on a few easily observable metrics to measure the effectiveness of this leadership training programme. One metric that they decide to monitor is the proportion of managers who stay with the company for three years. They hypothesize that a larger proportion of managers in the training group would remain with the company after three years. A second metric of interest is the average performance evaluation score of the employee for three years. They speculate that, on average, the managers in the training group would have a higher average performance score. A third metric they consider important is the average employee satisfaction (ESAT) score of the direct reports of a manager. They figure that the direct reports of those in the training group would have higher average ESAT scores. Armed with these three metrics and a knowledge of the Kirkpatrick framework, Roma believes she can convince Jim about a ballpark value of the leadership training programme.

Roma seeks an appointment with Jim the next week to discuss her proposal. Her feeling is that Jim was unenthusiastic about the programme and would hardly spare ten to fifteen minutes for her. She is even preparing mentally to send a few reminders to get the appointment. But, to her great surprise, she receives an immediate response and not only that, a full hour of Jim's time to discuss the programme. Roma feels this is most unusual. She wonders whether Jim has changed his opinion after the previous meeting. On the appointed day she prepares herself with a lot of material on the Kirkpatrick framework and her proposed method of tracking behavioural change. She creates a few scenarios to highlight possible cases. While the scenarios are mostly positive, some of the scenarios make her somewhat jittery. What if Jim latches on to one of them? How will she mitigate the risk of those scenarios? With no clear plan in mind, she decides to postpone a discussion on risk mitigation for a follow-up meeting.

Jim turns out to be very supportive of Roma's ideas in the meeting and appreciates her efforts to measure the impact of training. He doesn't even bother too much about the problematic scenarios, simply asking Roma to discuss with her team the possible steps to mitigate risks.

Towards the end of the meeting Jim raises two points that worry Roma—the first point is about the loyal employees and how to meet their career aspirations, and the second point is about the selection of managers for the leadership programme. The very fact that only some managers will get a chance to attend the programme may be perceived quite negatively by those who don't. They might feel that their career aspirations will not be met in this company and start looking for greener pastures. Thus, it will be quite natural to have higher attrition in the group that is not selected for this training. So, Roma's attrition metric may be positive simply because of this reason. How will Roma address this?

Roma calls Brij to know if he has faced such queries in the course of his work and how he dealt with them. Brij answers in the affirmative and says that the presence of confounding factors is a bane with any such observational study. While Jim thinks the impact of the training can create problems because of increased attrition in a certain group and not because of the training per se, Brij argues that a difficult job market, created by macroeconomic concerns, can greatly reduce attrition in both groups, which may falsely indicate that the training had no impact. Brij suggests that Roma set up a very transparent process of selection of managers for the training programme. The top management may be requested to step in to allay any fear of reduced career opportunities for the group not selected for the training. One may even consider alternative training arrangements for them. Regarding the impact of change in the business environment, one should remain open to the possibility of taking care of that at the analysis stage if a drastic change does indeed take place.

Roma updates Jim with the following plan. She will arrange an open examination for all new managers to judge their suitability for the leadership programme. The examination will be conducted by an independent organization which would also conduct the training. On the basis of their performance in the examination, the candidates would be shortlisted for personal interviews. The personal interview will be conducted by the training organization, but one senior executive of the company will also be on the panel to give the relevant inputs. Based on their performance in the interview, the final selection of the candidates will be made. The training organization will closely monitor the performance of the candidates during the programme and give periodic feedback. The company will arrange for another training programme for the loyal employees with different content. She proposes to monitor the performance of the training programme through the three metrics she had suggested. Moreover, she proposes to involve a consulting statistician to ensure that a proper analysis of the collected data is done and any significant change in the business environment is accounted for. Jim promptly suggests that she should involve the statistician before the programme starts as it is often difficult to get the correct data unless it is planned well in advance. Roma agrees to this. Jim also suggests that she start working on the leadership development programme for loyal employees immediately and that there should not be a big gap between the launch of these two programmes. While this is quite challenging for Roma, she decides to give it a shot.

At the end of this short meeting, Jim picks up the proposal papers and writes 'Go ahead. Hope the programme meets the objectives!' much to Roma's delight. She realizes that her first struggle has just ended, but she now faces the bigger challenge of successful implementation.

SUMMARY

Investing in talent through skill-enhancement trainings is a key component of any HR operations strategy. This not only serves to 'sharpen the saw', but also keeps employees engaged and motivated. While measuring return on investment is an arduous task, there are simple measures that one can employ to ascertain if the training has yielded any benefits.

CHAPTER 12

UNDERSTANDING WHY EMPLOYEES LEAVE

Shiva was returning home after another terrible day at office. Vikas, his manager, thought he was good for nothing and a work shirker. Any suggestion given by him was treated with disdain by Vikas who openly asked Shiva's colleagues to avoid his company. The genesis of this problem lay in the fact that in a team meeting with the senior management, around two months ago, Shiva told them about some of the problems he was facing at work and requested that he be sent for trainings relevant for the job. Vikas took this as a slight and an attempt by Shiva to show him and his leadership capability in a poor light before the senior management. He was further angered because the cost of the training would be debited from his unit. While he had already formulated a training plan that met the training goals of his unit at the lowest cost, incorporating Shiva's training was a big additional cost that would surely impact his performance report adversely. Since then he targeted Shiva and tried to isolate him in all activities. He delayed sanctioning his leave applications, gave him no raise in the annual performance review, and even gave him a poor appraisal rating, putting him in the lowest category of 'needs to immediately improve performance'. He joked to the others that Shiva would soon get 'only trainings and no work' and Shiva should be grateful to him for that. Shiva applied for a revision of his performance appraisal but had little hope that the senior management would allow a revision, given that Vikas had strongly opposed it. He was fed up with Vikas's hostile attitude and started applying to other companies.

The phone's vibration awoke Shiva from his slumber in the bus back home. The call was from a placement agency that had arranged his interview with a competitor firm the next day. Shiva knew that an important task needed to be completed at office the next day. He dithered for a few minutes, debating whether he should accept the interview opportunity. Sensing his dilemma, the placement counsellor, Neera, asked him whether he was serious about changing his job to which he replied 'Yes'. Then Neera asked him the reason for seeking a change to which he replied 'problems with my manager'. Neera commented on that saying, 'If your manager doesn't value your work, why are you trying to help him by missing out on this great opportunity?' That helped Shiva make up his mind quickly. He decided to attend the interview. He also decided to switch off his phone all day so that he didn't have to respond to Vikas's calls. 'If Vikas is so good, as he claims, he should be able to get the work done without me,' said Shiva to himself.

The interview went well for Shiva and his profile matched remarkably well with the requirements. The new company decided to offer him a 40 per cent raise in salary and offered to buy out his notice period. They gave him an offer letter within hours, which Shiva accepted on the spot. The next day Shiva resigned from his position, which caused quite a stir. He had served the company diligently for the last five years and was known as 'Mr Dependable' among his peers and seniors. Many thought that he loved the company so much that he would retire from it. The HR manager, Dipesh, called Shiva to know the reason behind his drastic action. Shiva narrated the difficulties he had been facing in the past few months with Vikas, the poor performance appraisal and no response from the management on his request for a review. Dipesh offered to sort this out quickly by transferring him to a new manager and arranging a raise of 20 per cent. Shiva politely declined the offer from Dipesh, knowing how companies renege on their promises after the employee withdraws his resignation letter.

For the company, Shiva's resignation was a considerable loss. It was difficult to get an employee of comparable quality and experience. Moreover, it was an expensive affair as the compensation offered needed to be attractive enough, and that would mean an increase of 50–75 per cent in cost. In addition, there would be a substantial training cost that would need to be incurred. Dipesh wondered whether he could have acted differently to avoid this situation.

ATTRITION MODELLING

A few weeks later, Dipesh attended a conference focusing on human resource development. In one of the sessions Prof. Ajeet from a leading institute discussed the important role analytics can play in the field of HR. After the session Dipesh discussed with Prof. Ajeet the problem of retaining talent and also the need for an early warning system that would alert the management that certain employees are likely to leave the company. Such an early warning system would allow time for the management to address the employee's grievances, thereby reducing his chances of leaving. Prof. Ajeet assured Dipesh that building such a system was possible if he had the requisite data. Dipesh asked what data was required to which Prof. Ajeet gave a tentative list. Dipesh said that at present not much of the data was available, but he may be able to capture the required data going forward. Prof. Ajeet asked him to meet him next week at his office to continue the discussion. In the meantime, he asked Dipesh to identify all the variables that he thought would have a bearing on an employee's decision to leave the company.

The next day in the office Dipesh called a meeting of a few select employees across different levels to try to understand why people leave. Different reasons were suggested by the group, including better salary, increments, better growth opportunities, better learning, job satisfaction, number of additional hours of work per week, family commitments, caring for a child, lack of flexible working hours, commuting time and availability and convenience of transportation. Dipesh then narrated Shiva's case and asked them which of these factors had contributed to Shiva's decision to leave the company after working there for five years. After a brief silence one member of the group said that she had heard from a colleague that Shiva was unhappy with this year's increment. Another member of the group chimed in quickly and attributed the no-increment decision to the politics being played by Vikas. He said that Shiva was having a bad time and he was visibly unhappy with the way Vikas was treating him. Dipesh said that Shiva had told him similar things during the mandatory exit interview. He was wondering how this could be captured in an objective manner. An enthusiastic new employee suggested a mechanism by which a colleague can report any such observations to the HR department. However, this was greeted with protest from the others as they felt that this would undermine trust and lead to more friction. Dipesh understood the concern for privacy but sought to know how such an important variable could be captured by the system.

Prof. Ajeet gave Dipesh an early-morning meeting appointment. Dipesh knew Prof. Ajeet was a busy man and so he wanted to make the most of his time. He made a short presentation on the problem and the possible factors identified in the meeting. He also wanted to mention which data were easily obtainable and which would be difficult to capture. He particularly wanted to discuss with the professor how to capture events such as the ones that led to Shiva's exit. As he entered Prof. Ajeet's office, the professor asked him, 'When do you plan to change your job?' Dipesh smiled and said, 'No plans as yet.' Prof. Ajeet asked, 'Is this your first job?' Dipesh explained that this was his third job and he had acquired ten years' experience before joining this company, and he had been in it for about two years. 'How did you land up here?' asked the professor. 'Well, my wife disliked being in Noida and wanted to go to Bengaluru. When this job offer came along she pressured me to take it. The remuneration was decent and she jumped at the prospect of shifting to Bengaluru. There was no other reason as such. I was doing quite well in the earlier company as well,' said Dipesh. Prof. Ajeet then queried Dipesh on how he would have predicted his own attrition. 'I left my first job because the salary was too low compared to the industry standard. The location was Mumbai, so after I got married it became very difficult to manage my finances. I had to seek a higher paying job which I got in Noida,' Dipesh explained. 'I guess family commitment plays an important role in my quitting decisions.'

FIGURE 12.1: Key Factors of Attrition Modelling

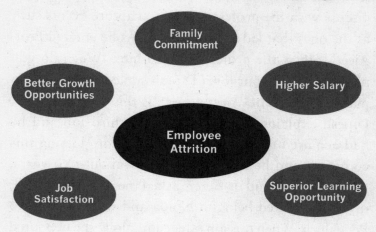

In the subsequent discussions, Prof. Ajeet stressed that the problem of predicting attrition was quite complex. It depended on a large number of variables, some easily quantifiable and some not. Measurement scales would have to be prepared for measuring the difficult ones like job satisfaction, relationship with the boss, family preference, etc. These variables would have to be measured at predetermined intervals, say, quarterly, and these values can be used in the attrition model. A logistic regression model can then be attempted to predict the probability of attrition in the next quarter or next two quarters, etc.

Dipesh asked the professor about the method of creating a measurement scale for a variable like job satisfaction. Prof. Ajeet replied that many such scales are available in the academic literature, but they need to be adapted to the Indian context. These are usually ordinal scales of the Likert variety. Respondents are asked to give their opinions and/or ratings on several items and then a summation of the scores is used for the purpose of measurement. It is important to check that the scale is measuring the correct quantity by doing a pre-test.

Prof. Ajeet repeatedly stressed the importance of accurate measurement of the identified variables for use in the model. He asked Dipesh to create an environment that would induce employees to respond to questionnaires truthfully, without the fear of any repercussions. Only then an accurate measurement of variables such as job satisfaction or relationship with the boss would be possible. Dipesh wondered if the very act of measuring these variables would have an impact on the behaviour of the employees and their bosses. He could also foresee considerable resistance among the middle managers regarding the measurement of some of these variables.

As he was leaving the professor's office, Dipesh asked for his help in analysing the data. Prof. Ajeet assured his help but signed off with 'Remember that good analysis requires good data. So focus on getting the right data.' Dipesh left his office thinking about what step to take next.

FIGURE 12.2: Four Types of Measurement Scales

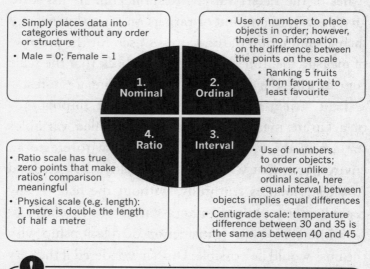

- Simply places data into categories without any order or structure
- Male = 0; Female = 1

- Use of numbers to place objects in order; however, there is no information on the difference between the points on the scale
  - Ranking 5 fruits from favourite to least favourite

1. Nominal

2. Ordinal

4. Ratio

3. Interval

- Ratio scale has true zero points that make ratios' comparison meaningful
- Physical scale (e.g. length): 1 metre is double the length of half a metre

- Use of numbers to order objects; however, unlike ordinal scale, here equal interval between objects implies equal differences
- Centigrade scale: temperature difference between 30 and 35 is the same as between 40 and 45

The attrition model's success depends heavily on the availability of internal and external data for analysis as well as the appropriate level and quality of the data. Companies must invest in building infrastructure to capture historical information to be readily available for future use.

YOU MUST ALSO KNOW

The methodology described above can be leveraged to predict attrition of any type, such as customer attrition in a wide variety of industries like retail stores, insurance companies and internet service providers, where the cost of losing a customer is substantial and customer attrition is the key metric impacting business performance.

NOTES

CHAPTER 1: IN THE EYES OF THE LENDER

1. For the details of the technique, see Daniel S. Putler and Robert E. Krider, *Customer and Business Analytics: Applied Data Mining for Business Decision Making Using R* (Florida: CRC Press, 2012), chapter 5.

CHAPTER 2: WHERE THE MONEY LIES

1. For a detailed discussion on these topics, please refer to Richard Brealey, Stewart Myers, Franklin Allen and Pitabas Mohanty, *Principles of Corporate Finance* (Noida: Tata McGraw Hill Education, 2007; 8th Edition).
2. See Monte Carlo method on Wikipedia at http://en.wikipedia.org/wiki/Monte_Carlo_method.
3. See Aparna Gupta, *Risk Management and Simulation* (CRC Press), chapter 4, for fuller details.

CHAPTER 3: IN THE WORLD OF RISKS

1. For more information on ISO, please visit www.iso.org.
2. See Bis.org, https://www.bis.org/about/index. htm?l=2&m=1%7C1.
3. For details see Michael Frenkel, Ulrich Hommel and Markus Rudolf (eds.), *Risk Management: Challenge and Opportunity* (New York: Springer, 2005; 2nd Edition), pp. 99–124.
4. See John C. Hull, *Risk Management and Financial Institutions* (Prentice Hall, 2009; 2nd Edition), chapter 18, for a detailed discussion on these topics.

CHAPTER 4: PUTTING YOUR EGGS IN DIFFERENT BASKETS

1. See David Freedman, Robert Pisani and Roger Purves, *Statistics* (New York: W.W. Norton & Company, 2007), chapter 8 on correlation and covariance.
2. For a detailed discussion on these, please refer to Richard Brealey, Stewart Myers, Franklin Allen and Pitabas Mohanty, *Principles of Corporate Finance* (Noida: Tata McGraw Hill Education, 2007; 8th Edition), chapter 8.

CHAPTER 7: PREDICTIVE MODELLING

1. See also chapter 1 and for details of the technique, see Daniel S. Putler and Robert E. Krider, *Customer and*

Business Analytics: Applied Data Mining for Business Decision Making Using R (Florida: CRC Press, 2012), chapter 5.

2. For details see Purba H. Rao, *Predictive Modelling in Strategic Marketing* (Delhi: Prentice Hall of India Learning, 2007; 11th Edition), chapter 5 and case studies.

CHAPTER 8: THE MARKETING MIX

1. The data and diagrams in this section have been derived from Gerard J. Tellis, 'Modeling Marketing Mix', in Rajiv Grover and Marco Vriens, *The Handbook of Marketing Research: Uses, Misuses, and Future Advances* (California: Sage Publications, 2006), pp. 506–22.

2. Gerard J. Tellis and Doyle Weiss, 'Does TV Advertising Really Affect Sales? The Role of Measures, Models and Data Aggregation', *Journal of Advertising Research* 24, No. 3, Fall 1995, pp. 1–12.

3. See David Freedman, Robert Pisani and Roger Purves, *Statistics* (New York: W.W. Norton & Company, 2007), chapter 12 for the details of this technique.

CHAPTER 9: TOO MUCH OR TOO LITTLE?

1. For a detailed discussion on the newsvendor model and continuous probability distribution, see Gerard Cachon and Christian Terweisch, 'Betting on Uncertain Demand:

The Newsvendor Model' (chapter 11), in *Matching Supply with Demand: Introduction to Operations Management* (2nd Edition).

2. Barry Smith, John F. Leimkuhler and Ross M. Darrow, 'Yield Management at American Airlines', *Interfaces* 22, No. 1, January–February 1992, pp. 8–31.

CHAPTER 10: IS THE PROCESS UNDER CONTROL?

1. See also Robert Stine and Dean Foster, *Statistics for Business: Decision Making and Analysis* (London: Pearson, 2010), chapter 14 on sampling variation and quality.

2. David Freedman, Robert Pisani and Roger Purves, *Statistics* (New York: W.W. Norton & Company, 2007), chapter 5 on normal distribution and its properties.

CHAPTER 11: INVESTING IN TALENT

1. The four-level training model was created by Donald Kirkpatrick, a professor at the University of Wisconsin, USA. *Transferring Learning to Behavior* and *Implementing the Four Levels* are some of his other well-known works on training evaluation.

A NOTE ON THE AUTHOR

Prof. Arnab Kumar Laha is a member of the faculty at the Indian Institute of Management, Ahmedabad. He received his PhD degree from the Indian Statistical Institute. He has a strong interest in the fields of business analytics, quality management and risk management and teaches several courses on these subjects at IIMA. He has published several research papers in national and international journals of repute.

Prof. Laha was featured among India's best business school professors by *Business Today* in 2006 and *Business India* in 2012. In August 2014, he was named as one of the '10 Most Prominent Analytics Academicians in India' by *Analytics India Magazine*. He is the convener of the IIMA series of conferences on Advanced Data Analysis, Business Analytics and

Intelligence, which is held biennially since 2009. He has been associated as a consultant with several reputed organizations, both in the private and public sectors.

A NOTE ON IIMA BUSINESS BOOKS

The IIM Ahmedabad Business Books series brings key
issues in management and business to a general audience.
With a wealth of information and illustrations from
contemporary Indian business, these non-academic and
user-friendly books from the faculty of IIM Ahmedabad
are essential corporate reading.

www.iimabooks.com

OTHER BOOKS IN THIS SERIES